ECCE ROMANI IA

A LATIN
READING PROGRAM

FOURTH EDITION

ECCE ROMANI IA

A LATIN
READING PROGRAM

FOURTH EDITION

Boston, Massachusetts
Glenview, Illinois
Shoreview, Minnesota
Parsippany, New Jersey
Upper Saddle River, New Jersey

This North American edition of *Ecce Romani* is based on *Ecce Romani: A Latin Reading Course*, originally prepared by The Scottish Classics Group © copyright The Scottish Classics Group 1971, 1982, and published in the United Kingdom by Oliver and Boyd, a division of Longman Group.

Photo Credits appear on page 173, which constitutes an extension of this copyright page.

Cover illustration: Lin Wang
Text art: Lin Wang
Maps: John Burgoyne

13-digit ISBN: 978-0-13-361092-5
10-digit ISBN: 0-13-361092-6

16   17

Series Editor: Gilbert Lawall
Professor Emeritus of Classics
University of Massachusetts, Amherst, Massachusetts

AUTHORS AND CONSULTANTS

Timothy S. Abney
Marquette High School
Chesterfield, Missouri

Jim Bigger
McLean High School
McLean, Virginia

Melissa Schons Bishop
Windermere, Florida

Peter C. Brush
Deerfield Academy
Deerfield, Massachusetts

Penny R. Cipolone
Gateway Regional High School
Woodbury Heights, New Jersey

Gail A. Cooper
Academy of the New Church
Bryn Athyn, Pennsylvania

Sally Davis
Arlington Public Schools
Arlington, Virginia

Pauline P. Demetri
Cambridge Rindge & Latin
School
Cambridge, Massachusetts

Dennis De Young
Montgomery Bell Academy
Nashville, Tennessee

Katy Ganino
Wayland Middle School
Wayland, Massachusetts

Jane Hall
National Latin Exam
Alexandria, Virginia

Sally Hatcher
Winsor School
Boston, Massachusetts

Thalia Pantelidis Hocker
Old Dominion University
Norfolk, Virginia

Anthony L.C. Hollingsworth
Roger Williams University
Bristol, Rhode Island

Dexter Hoyos
Sydney University
Sydney, Australia

Joan C. Jahnige
Kentucky Educational Television
Lexington, Kentucky

Caroline Switzer Kelly
Covenant Day School
Charlotte, North Carolina

Glenn M. Knudsvig
University of Michigan
Ann Arbor, Michigan

Richard A. LaFleur
University of Georgia
Athens, Georgia

Shirley G. Lowe
Wayland Public Schools
Wayland, MA

Maureen O'Donnell
W.T. Woodson High School
Fairfax, Virginia

Ronald B. Palma
Holland Hall School
Tulsa, Oklahoma

David J. Perry
Rye High School
Rye, New York

Kathleen M. Robinson
Harbor Day School
Corona del Mar, CA

Debra Pennell Ross
University of Michigan
Ann Arbor, Michigan

Andrew Schacht
St. Luke's School
New Canaan, Connecticut

Judith Lynn Sebesta
University of South Dakota
Vermillion, South Dakota

The Scottish Classics Group
Edinburgh, Scotland

David M. Tafe
Rye Country Day School
Rye, New York

Rex Wallace
University of Massachusetts
Amherst, Massachusetts

Allen Ward
University of Connecticut
Storrs, Connecticut

Elizabeth Lyding Will
Amherst College
Amherst, Massachusetts

Philip K. Woodruff
Lake Forest High School
Lake Forest, Illinois

CONTENTS

REFERENCE MATERIALS

MAPS

INTRODUCTION

Ecce Romani

The title of this series of Latin books is *Ecce Romani*, which means "Look! The Romans!" The books in the series will present the Romans to you as you learn the Latin language that they spoke. At first you will meet the members of a Roman family. As you continue reading, you will meet mythological and historical characters that meant much to the Romans and remain part of our cultural heritage today. You will be introduced to a vast and colorful world of ancient Mediterranean and European civilizations that included peoples who spoke many different languages, and you will meet people of many different cultures and social levels, ranging from slaves to emperors. You will read passages from many ancient Roman writers and thus come into direct communication with the ancient Romans themselves.

A Roman Family

Within this vast world, the focus of your attention will be the daily life of a typical upper-class Roman family, consisting of a father named Cornelius, a mother named Aurelia, a son named Marcus, a daughter named Cornelia, and a young boy named Sextus, who is a ward of the family. You will follow the development of Marcus and Cornelia from late childhood to the beginning of their lives as mature Romans.

Baiae

The Latin stories you will be reading about this family take place in A.D. 80, the year following the destruction of Pompeii by the eruption of Mount Vesuvius. The family lives in the great metropolis of Rome, but when you first meet them it is summertime, and they are living at their country home near Baiae in Campania (see map on page xiii).

Baiae, on the Bay of Naples, was a fashionable resort for wealthy Romans, many of whom built splendid country houses or villas there. The shoreline of the Bay of Naples was ringed with villas built on terraces so that their inhabitants could enjoy the beauty of the sparkling waves and the steep cliffs of the islands in the bay. On the terraces the Romans planted gardens and cool arbors of trees under which they could refresh themselves in the heat of the day. Along the shore they built fish ponds, which were flushed daily by the tides.

While the family is at Baiae, you will learn about a number of aspects of Roman culture, such as the family, dress, slavery, names, and life on country estates. When the family returns to Rome, your awareness of Roman culture will expand as you learn about life in the city and life on the frontiers of the Roman empire. You will experience some of the highlights of the cultural life of the city, such as the chariot races and the games in the Colosseum; you will see Cornelius and Aurelia, the parents in our family, fulfill their obligations to society; and you will follow the passage of their children, Marcus and Cornelia, through the rituals of coming of age and marriage. Latin passages adapted from

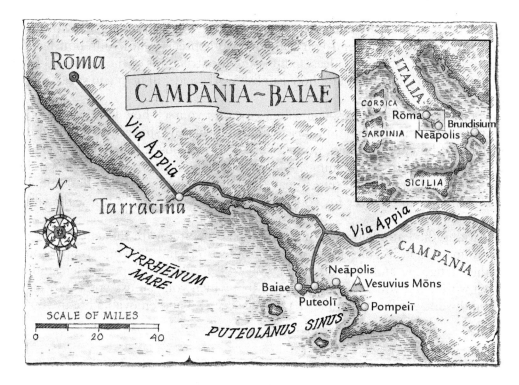

ancient authors in *The Romans Speak for Themselves*, a reader that accompanies *Ecce Romani*, will allow you to hear what the Romans themselves had to say about many of these aspects of their cultural life. All along the way you will have abundant opportunities to compare the cultural life of the Romans with our own today.

The Latin Language

As you read stories about the Roman family in this book, you will be learning Latin, a language that gave birth to a number of languages that are still used today, including Spanish, Portuguese, French, Italian, and Romanian. These modern languages are known as Romance languages, because they come from the language used by the ancient Romans.

In addition, even though the English language developed out of Germanic dialects, as much as sixty percent of English vocabulary comes directly or indirectly from Latin. Many French words of Latin origin were introduced into English by the Normans, a French people who conquered the English in 1066. Many other words of Latin origin came into English during the revival of classical learning in the Renaissance and Enlightenment (1550 and following), and Latin words have come and continue to come into English usage in scientific, medical, and legal terminology. The connections you will make between Latin words and English words will enhance your understanding of English vocabulary, especially of its larger, polysyllabic words. By connecting English words with their Latin roots, you will increase your ability to use English words correctly and effectively.

As you begin to read the Latin stories in this book, you will notice many differences between English and Latin, and you will come to appreciate how different languages have unique ways of expressing ideas. Comparing the structures of the Latin and English languages will help you understand how English works and will help you speak and write it better.

As you read the Latin stories, you will discover for yourself how Latin works as a language and how to understand and translate it. Following the stories you will find formal explanations of how the language works. These explanations will help you visualize the way Latin sentences express meaning, and they will help you learn the elements or building blocks of the language. Be sure to pay close attention as you read the Latin stories themselves and try to discover for yourself as much as you can about how the language works.

In learning the Latin language, in becoming acquainted with the cultural life of the ancient Romans, and in constantly making connections and drawing comparisons between their language and life and yours, you will develop a deeper understanding of your own world, and you will find many ways in which you can use your knowledge of Latin and the ancient Romans to lead a more successful and enjoyable life in your own world.

A Note on Vocabulary

You will encounter many Latin words as you read the stories and do the exercises in *Ecce Romani*. You will not need to learn all of them to the same degree. In the vocabulary lists below the stories and below some of the exercises, some of the Latin words are printed in boldface and some are not. You should acquire an active knowledge of the

The beautiful region of Latium has inspired artists over the centuries. The Roman Campagna with the Claudian Aqueduct, *oil on canvas, 1827, Jean-Baptiste-Camille Corot*

words in boldface. This means that you should be able to give the meaning of the Latin word when you see it in a story or a sentence and that you should also be able to give the Latin word when you see its English equivalent. You will also need to learn other information about these words. These words are for *mastery*. Other words in the vocabulary lists below the stories and below some of the exercises are not in boldface. For these words, you need only recognize the word when you see it and be able to give its meaning. These are words for *recognition*. You must be sure that you learn these words well enough to remember their English meanings when you see them again in stories and sentences. In learning Latin from *Ecce Romani*, you will acquire a rich Latin vocabulary as you read stories about the members of our Roman family in a variety of situations. The distinction we make between words for mastery and words for recognition will make it easier for you to enjoy a wealth of detail and local color in the stories without requiring you to master an excessive number of Latin words.

Go Online

Every chapter of your book contains Web Codes that allow you to Go Online to the *Ecce Romani* Companion Web Site. This Web Site contains activities for additional practice with vocabulary, grammar, and culture and a Self-Test that corresponds to the Review sections in your book. In order to Go Online, go to www.PHSchool.com, type in the Web Code you would like to access, and click on the yellow arrow.

In order to access additional information and links that will be useful to you throughout the year, use the following Web Code:

Go Online
PHSchool.com
Web Code: jfd-0001

Italia

SCALE OF MILES
0   75   150

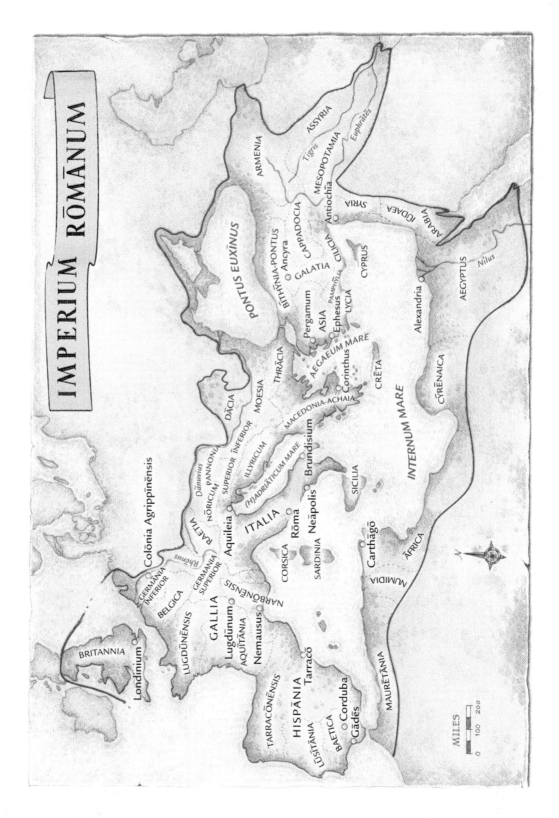

TWO ROMAN GIRLS

Look! There's a girl in the picure, named Corneilia!

Ecce! In pictūrā est puella, nōmine Cornēlia. Cornēlia est puella Rōmāna quae in Italiā habitat. Etiam in pictūrā est vīlla rūstica ubi Cornēlia aestāte habitat. *also in the pic is her countryhome and farm cornellia* Cornēlia est laeta quod iam in vīllā habitat. Cornēlia iam sub arbore sedet et legit. *Cornelia is happy in her canty home — Cornelia now is under the tree and sitting reading.* Etiam in pictūrā est altera puella, nōmine Flāvia. Flāvia est puella Rōmāna quae in vīllā vīcīnā habitat. Dum Cornēlia legit, Flāvia scrībit. Laeta est Flāvia quod Cornēlia iam in 5 vīllā habitat. *While Cornelia reads, Flavia writes. Flavia is happy because Corneilia now*

- 1 **Ecce!** *Look!*
- **puella,** *(a/the) girl*
- **nōmine,** *by name, named*
- **quae,** *who*
- 2 **habitat,** *(she/he) lives, is living, does live*
- **etiam,** *also*
- **vīlla,** *(a/the) country house*
  - **vīlla rūstica,** *(a/the) country house and farm*
- **ubi,** *where*
- **aestāte,** *in the summer*
- 3 **laeta,** *happy*

- **quod,** *because*
- **iam,** *now*
- **sub arbore,** *under the tree*
- **sedet,** *(she/he) sits, is sitting, does sit*
- **et,** *and*
- **legit,** *(she/he) reads, is reading, does read*
- 4 **altera,** *second, another*
- 5 **vīcīna,** *neighboring*
- **dum,** *while*
- **scrībit,** *(she/he) writes, is writing, does write*

N.B. Latin does not have articles (*a, an, the*), and so **puella** can mean either *a girl* or *the girl.*

Latin verbs can be translated several ways, e.g., **habitat** can be translated *(she/he) lives, is living,* or *does live.*

EXERCISE 1a

Respondē Latīnē:

1. Quis est Cornēlia?
2. Ubi habitat Cornēlia?
3. Cūr est Cornēlia laeta?
4. Quid facit Cornēlia?
5. Ubi habitat Flāvia?
6. Quid facit Flāvia?
7. Cūr est Flāvia laeta?

Quis...? *Who...?*

Cūr...? *Why...?*
Quid facit...? *What is...doing? What does...do?*

Parts of Speech: Nouns, Adjectives, and Verbs

When learning Latin you will be learning how language expresses meaning, and you will need to know certain grammatical terms so that you can talk about how Latin does this. The most important terms are those for the parts of speech, the basic building blocks of meaning in sentences. The most important parts of speech are:

> **nouns:** names of persons, places, things, qualities, or acts;
> **adjectives:** words that describe persons, places, things, qualities, or acts;
> **verbs:** words that denote actions (e.g., *sits*) or existence (e.g., *is*).

In the story on page 3, the words **pictūrā** (1), **Cornēlia** (1), and **Italiā** (2) are nouns; the words **Rōmāna** (1), **rūstica** (2), and **laeta** (3) are adjectives; and the words **est** (1), **habitat** (2), and **sedet** (3) are verbs.

nt - alwas plural

Vergil holds a scroll open to line 8 of the *Aeneid*.
Mosaic, Tunis, early third century A.D.

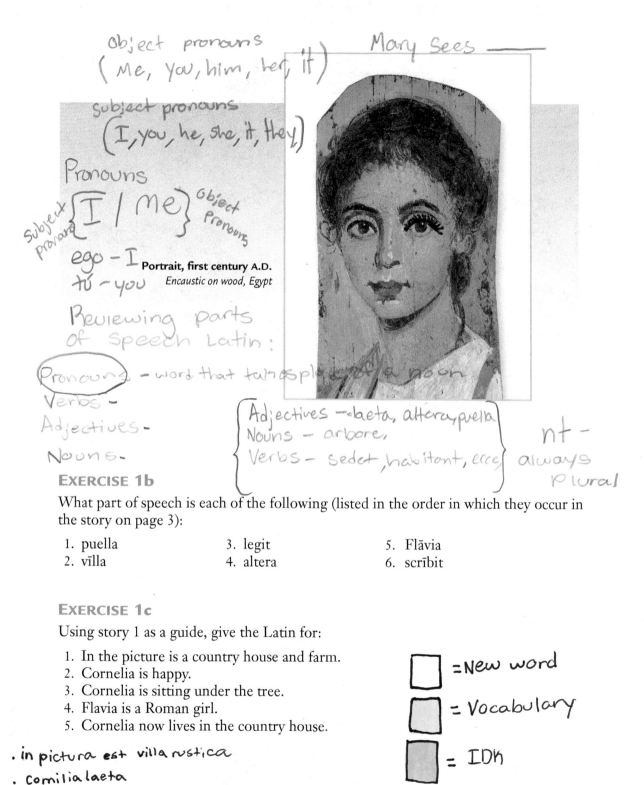

Handwritten notes:

Object pronouns
(me, you, him, her, it)

Mary sees ___

subject pronouns
(I, you, he, she, it, they)

Pronouns

Subject pronoun {I / me} Object Pronouns

ego - I
tú - you

Portrait, first century A.D.
Encaustic on wood, Egypt

Reviewing parts of speech Latin:

Pronouns - word that takes place of a noun
Verbs -
Adjectives -
Nouns -

Adjectives - laeta, altera, puella
Nouns - arbore,
Verbs - sedet, habitant, ecce

nt - always plural

EXERCISE 1b

What part of speech is each of the following (listed in the order in which they occur in the story on page 3):

1. puella
2. vīlla
3. legit
4. altera
5. Flāvia
6. scrībit

EXERCISE 1c

Using story 1 as a guide, give the Latin for:

1. In the picture is a country house and farm.
2. Cornelia is happy.
3. Cornelia is sitting under the tree.
4. Flavia is a Roman girl.
5. Cornelia now lives in the country house.

□ = New word

▨ = Vocabulary

▨ = IDK

Handwritten answers:

- in pictura est villa rustica
- Comilia laeta
- Comielia sedet sub abore
- Flavia est ~~romana~~ puella Romana
- Comielia iam in villa habitat

A SUMMER AFTERNOON

Cornēlia est puella Rōmāna. Flāvia quoque est puella Rōmāna. Cornēlia et Flāvia sunt puellae Rōmānae quae in Italiā habitant. Cornēlia et Flāvia sunt amīcae. Hodiē puellae nōn sedent sed in agrīs ambulant. Brevī tempore Cornēlia dēfessa est. Nōn iam ambulat sed sub arbore sedet. Flāvia, quae est puella strēnua, in agrīs currit. Brevī tempore Flāvia quoque est dēfessa. Iam Flāvia et Cornēlia sub arbore sedent quod dēfessae sunt. Dum puellae sub arbore sedent, Cornēlia legit et Flāvia scrībit. Tandem puellae ex agrīs ad vīllam rūsticam lentē ambulant.

5

1 **quoque,** adv., *also*
2 **sunt,** *(they) are*
  amīcae, *friends*
3 **hodiē,** adv., *today*
  sed, conj., *but*
  in agrīs, *in the fields*
  ambulant, *(they) walk, are walking,*
    do walk
  brevī tempore, *in a short time, soon*
  dēfessa, *tired*

4 **nōn iam,** adv., *no longer*
  strēnua, *active, energetic*
  currit, *(she/he) runs, is running,*
    does run
6 **tandem,** adv., *at last*
7 **ex agrīs,** *from/out of the fields*
  ad vīllam rūsticam, *to/toward the*
    country house and farm
  lentē, adv., *slowly*

EXERCISE 2a

Respondē Latīnē:

1. Ubi habitant Cornēlia et Flāvia?
2. Quid faciunt puellae hodiē?
3. Quid facit Cornēlia quod dēfessa est?
4. Quid faciunt puellae sub arbore?

Quid faciunt…? *What are…doing?*
           What do…do?

BUILDING THE MEANING

Subjects, Verbs, Linking Verbs, and Complements

Subjects and *verbs* are core elements of sentences. It is important to identify them as you meet them in Latin sentences. You may mark subjects (the person or thing that *is* or *does something*) with the letter S and verbs with the letter V:

|S   V| |S   V|
|Cornēlia **est** puella Rōmāna.| |Puellae in Italiā **habitant.**|

The verb **est** is used as a *linking verb* (LV) when it links the subject with a noun or an adjective. This noun or adjective completes the pattern of the sentence and is called a *complement* (C):

|S   LV   C| |S   LV   C|
|Cornēlia **est** puella.| |Flāvia **est** dēfessa.|

These sentences may also be written as follows with no change in meaning:

|S   C   LV| |S   C   LV|
|Cornēlia puella **est.**| |Flāvia dēfessa **est.**|

When **est** and **sunt** appear before the subject and there is no complement, they are normally translated *there is* and *there are*:

In pictūrā **est** puella. (1:1)   In pictūrā **sunt** puellae.
There is *a girl in the picture.*   ***There are*** *girls in the picture.*

FORMS

Go Online
PHSchool.com
Web Code: jfd-0002

Verbs: The Endings -*t* and -*nt*

Look at these sentences:

1. Cornēlia es**t** puella Rōmāna.
   Cornelia is a Roman girl.
2. Puella in agrīs curri**t** quod laeta es**t**.
   The girl is running in the fields because she is happy.
3. Cornēlia et Flāvia su**nt** puellae Rōmānae.
   Cornelia and Flavia are Roman girls.
4. Puellae in agrīs curru**nt** quod laetae su**nt**.
   The girls are running in the fields because they are happy.

Girls playing a ball game
Fragment of a Roman relief, second century A.D.

If the subject is singular (e.g., **Cornēlia** and **puella** in the first two sentences), the verb ends in *-t*.

If the subject is plural (e.g., **Cornēlia et Flāvia** and **puellae** in the third and fourth sentences), the verb ends in *-nt*.

You have noticed that vocabulary lists give definitions of verbs as follows: **sedet**, *(she/he) sits, is sitting, does sit*. Verbs may be used with a noun as subject, as in the sentence **Brevī tempore <u>Cornēlia</u> dēfessa est** (line 3 in the story at the beginning of this chapter). If there is no stated subject, as in the sentence **Nōn iam ambulat sed sub arbore sedet**, you must include a pronoun when you translate: thus, *She no longer walks but sits under a tree.* Cornelia continues to be the subject since there is nothing in the sentence to indicate a change of subject.

EXERCISE 2b

Read these fragments of sentences and decide which word at the right best completes each sentence. Then read aloud and translate:

1. Flāvia in vīllā vīcīnā _____.   habitat/habitant
2. Cornēlia et Flāvia sub arbore _____.   sedet/sedent
3. Cornēlia et Flāvia dēfessae _____.   est/sunt
4. Flāvia strēnua _____.   est/sunt
5. Cornēlia et Flāvia sunt _____.   puella Rōmāna/puellae Rōmānae
6. Puellae in agrīs nōn iam _____.   currit/currunt

EXERCISE 2c

Read aloud, mentally noting subjects, verbs, and complements as you read. Note which verbs are linking verbs. Then translate:

Cornēlia est puella Rōmāna quae in vīllā rūsticā aestāte habitat. In vīllā vīcīnā habitat altera puella, nōmine Flāvia, quae est amīca eius. Dum puellae in vīllīs habitant, in agrīs saepe ambulant. Hodiē Cornēlia ad vīllam vīcīnam ambulat ubi in agrīs sub arbore sedet Flāvia. Iam puellae laetae currunt. Brevī tempore, quod dēfessae sunt, nōn iam currunt sed sub arbore sedent.

2 **eius**, *her*   **vīllīs**, *country houses*   3 **saepe**, adv., *often*

In the passage above, how many singular verbs can you find? How many plural verbs?

EXERCISE 2d

Using story 2 as a guide, give the Latin for:

1. Cornelia and Flavia live in Italy.
2. Cornelia and Flavia are walking in the fields.
3. Flavia is running.
4. In a short time the girls are tired and sit under a tree.
5. At last the girls walk slowly to the country house.

Go Online
PHSchool.com
Web Code: jfd-0002

A ROMAN FAMILY

In our family, there is a daughter, Cornelia, who is fourteen, a son, Marcus, sixteen, a father, Gaius Cornelius, and a mother, Aurelia. At the **vīlla,** the education of the children is in the hands of their parents and a Greek slave, Eucleides.

The family of Cornelius traces its lineage far back in Roman history. One of the most distinguished members of the family was Publius Cornelius Scipio Africanus, the Roman general who defeated the Carthaginians in North Africa in the Second Punic War (218–201 B.C.). His daughter, Cornelia, was one of the most famous Roman women of all time and was the mother of the Gracchi brothers, who were great social reformers in the second century B.C. As our Cornelia sits under the tree, she is reading about her namesake in a book given to her by Eucleides, and she is wondering whether she too will become as famous as the Cornelia of old.

Cornelia, mother of the Gracchi, pointing to her sons as her treasures
Cornelia, Mother of the Gracchi, *oil on canvas, 1795, Joseph-Benoît Suvée*

Cornelius is responsible for the estate. As father, he is not only master of his own house, but he legally has power of life and death over his household, although he never exercises it. Aurelia runs the household and teaches her daughter what she will need to know when she gets married and has to run her own household. Aurelia and Cornelia do some wool-spinning and weaving but there are a number of slaves to help with the chores.

The family has living with it a twelve-year-old boy, Sextus, who used to live in Pompeii, where his mother died in the eruption of Mount Vesuvius the year before our story begins. Sextus's father is now on service overseas in Asia Minor, and he has left his son in Italy under the guardianship of his friend Cornelius.

Cornelia's friend Flavia lives in a neighboring country house.

Cornelia with her sons Tiberius and Gaius
Sculpture, Pierre-Jules Cavelier

ADDITIONAL READING:
The Romans Speak for Themselves: Book I: "The Family in Roman Society," pages 1–8.

notice! Masculine

IN THE GARDEN

In pictūrā est puer Rōmānus, nōmine Mārcus, quī in vīllā rūsticā habitat. Etiam in pictūrā est alter puer, nōmine Sextus, quī in eādem vīllā rūsticā habitat. Mārcus et Sextus sunt amīcī. Hodiē puerī in hortō clāmant et rīdent quod laetī sunt.

Vir quoque est in pictūrā, nōmine Dāvus, quī est servus. In Italiā sunt multī servī quī in agrīs et in vīllīs rūsticīs labōrant. Puerī sunt Rōmānī, sed Dāvus nōn est Rōmānus. Est 5 vir Britannicus quī iam in Italiā labōrat. Sextus et Mārcus, quod sunt puerī Rōmānī, nōn labōrant. Dāvus sōlus labōrat, īrātus quod puerī clāmant et in hortō currunt.

Subitō statua in piscīnam cadit. Sextus rīdet. Mārcus quoque rīdet, sed Dāvus, "Abīte, molestī!" clāmat et ad piscīnam īrātus currit. Puerī ex hortō currunt. Dāvus gemit.

1 **puer,** *(a/the) boy*
   quī, *who*   *Statua = Statue*
2 **eādem,** *the same*
3 **in hortō,** *in the garden*
   clāmant, *(they) shout, are shouting*
   rīdent, *(they) laugh, are laughing, smile*
4 **vir,** *(a/the) man*
   servus, *(a/the) slave*
   multī, *many*

5 **in vīllīs rūsticīs,** *in country houses*
   labōrant, *(they) work, are working*
7 **sōlus,** *alone*
   īrātus, *angry*
8 **subitō,** *adv., suddenly*
   in piscīnam, *into the fishpond*
   cadit, *(he/she/it) falls*
   Abīte, molestī! *Go away, pests!*
9 **gemit,** *(he/she) groans*

Latin words and phrases that are not printed in boldface are for recognition and not for mastery. See Introduction, pages xiv–xv.

EXERCISE 3a

Respondē Latīnē:

1. Quis est Sextus?
2. Suntne Mārcus et Sextus amīcī?
3. Quid faciunt puerī hodiē?
4. Quis est Dāvus?
5. Estne Mārcus servus?
6. Cūr est Dāvus īrātus?
7. Quid in piscīnam cadit?
8. Quid faciunt puerī?

-ne indicates a yes or no question

Minimē! *No!*
Ita vērō! *Yes!*

Nouns and Adjectives: Singular and Plural

Note how these nouns change from singular to plural:

Singular	Plural
puell*a*	puell*ae*
serv*us*	serv*ī*
puer	puer*ī*
vir	vir*ī*

Study the following sentences, and note how the nouns and adjectives change from singular to plural:

1. Cornēlia est **puell*a* Rōmān*a***.
   Cornēlia et Flāvia sunt **puell*ae* Rōmān*ae***.

2. Dāvus est **serv*us***.
   Mult*ī* serv*ī* in agrīs labōrant.

3. Mārcus est **puer Rōmān*us***.
   Mārcus et Sextus sunt **puer*ī* Rōmān*ī***.

4. Cornēlius est **vir Rōmān*us***.
   Vir*ī* Rōmān*ī* in Italiā habitant.

Pompeii

EXERCISE 3b

Change singulars
to plurals:

1. amīcus Rōmānus
2. puer sōlus
3. amīca laeta
4. servus dēfessus
5. puella īrāta
6. vir sōlus
7. vīlla rūstica
8. puer dēfessus
9. pictūra Rōmāna
10. vir laetus

Hortus with ***piscīna*** and ***porticus***
Villa of Julia Felix, Pompeii

EXERCISE 3c

Change plurals to singulars:

1. amīcae dēfessae
2. servī īrātī
3. puellae Rōmānae
4. virī dēfessī
5. vīllae vīcīnae
6. amīcī laetī
7. puellae strēnuae
8. virī Rōmānī
9. puellae īrātae
10. puerī sōlī
11. vīllae Rōmānae
12. servī dēfessī

EXERCISE 3d

Based on what you know about singular and plural forms of subjects, verbs, and adjectives, select the correct word or phrase to complete each sentence. Then read aloud and translate:

1. Mārcus et Sextus in eādem vīllā _____.   habitat/habitant
2. Dāvus vir Britannicus _____.   est/sunt
3. In agrīs labōrant _____.   servus/servī
4. Puerī et puellae saepe _____.   gemit/currit/currunt
5. Sunt in agrīs multī _____.   puella/servus/servī
6. In Italiā habitat _____.   Mārcus et Sextus/Mārcus/puellae
7. Mārcus et Sextus sunt puerī _____.   Rōmānus/Rōmānī/Rōmānae
8. Cornēlia et Flāvia sunt puellae _____.   Rōmānus/Rōmānī/Rōmānae
9. Aurēlia est fēmina _____.   Rōmānus/Rōmānī/Rōmāna

fēmina, *(a/the) woman*

EXERCISE 3e

Using stories 2 and 3 as guides, give the Latin for:

1. Today the boy is laughing because he is happy.
2. The tired girls are sitting under a tree.
3. In Italy many slaves work in country houses.
4. In the picture Cornelia is reading and Flavia is writing.
5. While Davus runs to the fishpond, the boys suddenly run out of the garden.

Roman interest in the different cultures of their empire is shown in this bust of a Syrian slave.
Bronze and lead decoration, Rome, second century A.D.

Roman Life II

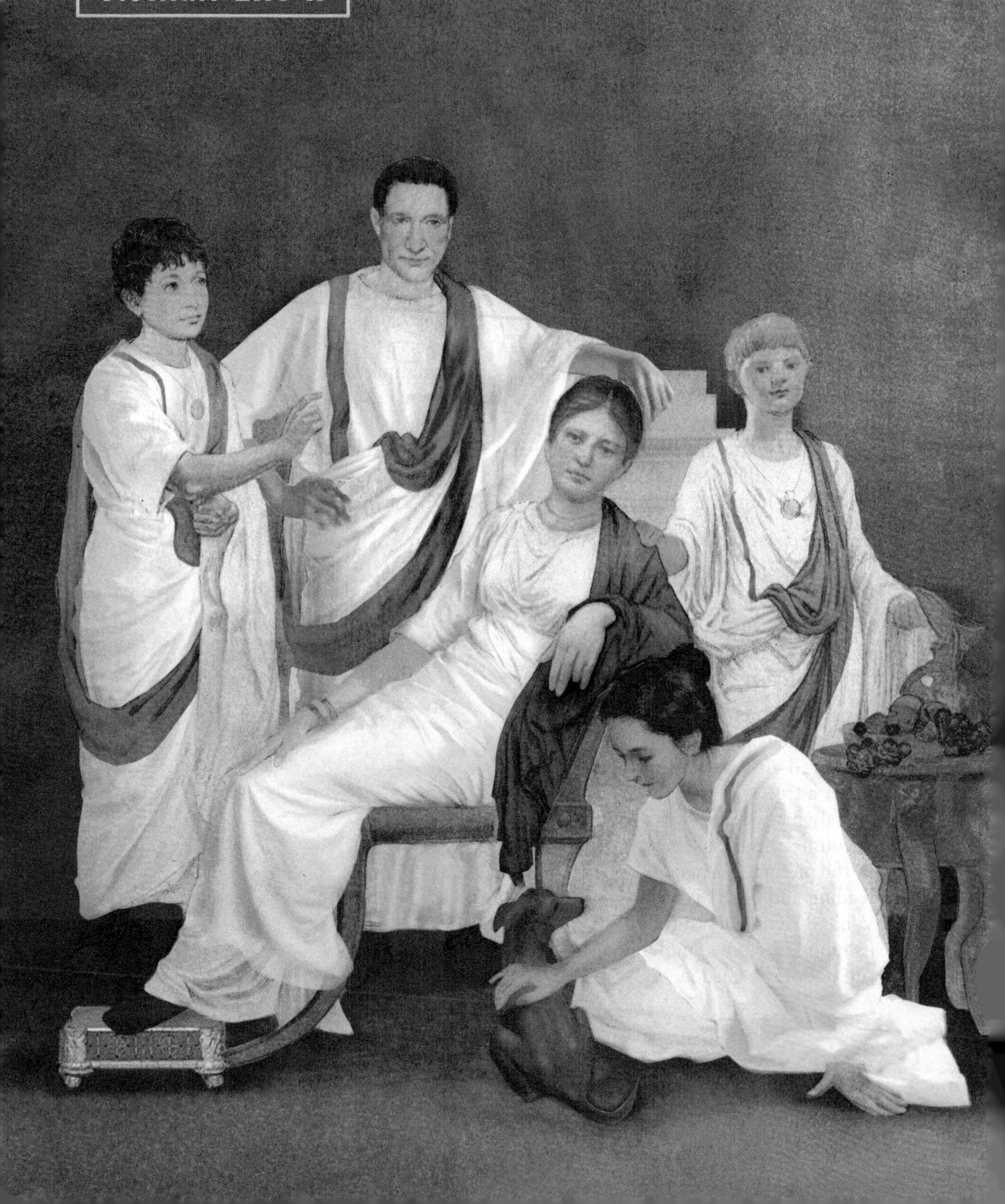

Go Online
PHSchool.com
Web Code: jfd-0003

DRESS

When formally dressed, the clothing of a Roman indicated his or her citizenship and status in the multicultural society of the Roman world. The picture opposite shows Cornelius's family and Sextus, the boy who is presently living with the family, all in formal dress. When living at their country villa, they would not always wear such formal attire.

Aurelia wears a simple blue tunic (**tunica**) with sleeves. Over the tunic, she wears a **stola**, a floor-length strapped dress without sleeves. The **stola** indicates that she is both a Roman citizen and the wife of a Roman citizen. She is shown here wearing a dark blue **palla** as well, a single, rectangular piece of material draped over her left shoulder. It could also be put around her body or over her head. She would wear this when out of doors.

Cornelius wears a knee-length tunic. To show that he is a senator, his tunic has broad purple stripes running from near each side of the neck down the front and down the back. On formal occasions in the country and always in the city, he wears a **toga** over his tunic. The toga indicates that he is a Roman citizen. Most Roman men would wear a plain white toga (**toga pūra**), also called a **toga virīlis** (*toga of manhood*), but since Cornelius has held a high magistracy, he wears a toga with a purple border (**toga praetexta**) to signify his rank.

Marcus and Sextus wear tunics with purple stripes that are narrower than those on Cornelius's tunic. Roman boys, before coming of age between fourteen and sixteen, wore the **toga praetexta** with purple border like the toga worn by high government officials. Suspended from their necks, Marcus and Sextus wear a golden **bulla**, a locket containing an amulet or charm to ward off evil and protect them from harm. A boy's father placed a **bulla** around his son's neck at the naming ceremony soon after the boy's birth, and the boy would wear the **bulla** until he came of age. At that time, he would dedicate his **bulla** and the first shavings of his beard to the household gods, the **Larēs** and **Penātēs**, and he would then put on the **toga virīlis**.

Cornelia wears a white tunic like the white ones worn by Marcus and Sextus but without the purple stripes, and she wears the **toga praetexta** to show her status as a Roman citizen. She will dedicate her **toga praetexta** to the goddess of maidenly virtue (**Fortūna Virginālis**) when she marries. Roman girls did not wear a **bulla**.

The footgear shown in the picture is more formal than the simple sandals (**soleae**) that all members of the family would wear when at leisure in the country house and fields.

A MISCHIEF-MAKER

Sextus est puer molestus quī semper Cornēliam vexat. Cornēlia igitur Sextum nōn amat. Hodiē sub arbore dormit Cornēlia. Sextus puellam cōnspicit et fūrtim appropinquat. Arborem ascendit et subitō magnā vōce clāmat. Vōcem Cornēlia audit sed Sextum nōn videt. Magna vōx Cornēliam terret. Sollicita est.

Tum Mārcus ad arborem currit. Mārcus puerum molestum cōnspicit et clāmat, "Dēscende, Sexte!"

Sextus clāmat, "Mārce, cūr tū nōn arborem ascendis? Nihil mē terret. Quid tē terret?"

"Cavē, Sexte!" clāmat Mārcus. "Rāmī sunt īnfirmī."

Subitō Mārcus et Cornēlia magnum fragōrem audiunt; Sextus ex arbore cadit. Rīdent Mārcus et Cornēlia, sed nōn rīdet Sextus.

1 **molestus,** *troublesome, annoying*
  semper, adv., *always*
  vexat, *(he/she) annoys*
  igitur, conj., *therefore*
2 **amat,** *(he/she) likes, loves*
  dormit, *(he/she) sleeps*
  cōnspicit, *(he/she) catches sight of*
  fūrtim, adv., *stealthily*
3 **appropinquat,** *(he/she) approaches*
  ascendit, *(he/she) climbs*
  magnus, *big, great*
    magnā vōce, *in a loud voice*
4 **audit,** *(he/she) hears, listens to*

  videt, *(he/she) sees*
  vōx, *(a/the) voice*
  terret, *(he/she/it) frightens*
  sollicita, *anxious, worried*
5 **tum,** adv., *at that moment, then*
6 **Dēscende, Sexte!** *Come down, Sextus!*
7 **tū,** *you (subject)*
  nihil, *nothing*
  tē, *you (direct object)*
8 **Cavē!** *Be careful!*
  rāmus, *(a/the) branch*
  īnfirmus, *weak, shaky*
9 **fragor,** *(a/the) crash, noise*

In Latin, the form **Sexte** is used when Sextus is addressed by name. (Compare **Mārce.**) No such change is made in English.

EXERCISE 4a

Respondē Latīnē:

1. Quālis puer est Sextus?
2. Quid facit Cornēlia hodiē?
3. Quid facit Sextus?
4. Quid audit Cornēlia?
5. Quō Mārcus currit?
6. Quid clāmat Sextus?
7. Quid audiunt Mārcus et Cornēlia?

Quālis…? *What sort of…?*

Quō…? *Where…to?*

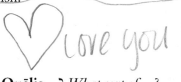
Go Online
PHSchool.com
Web Code: jfd-0004

Review

Select, read aloud, and translate:

1. Mārcus est puer _____.
2. Flāvia et Cornēlia in hortō _____.
3. Mārcus et Sextus sunt _____.
4. Mārcus nōn est _____.
5. Puerī nōn sunt _____.
6. Mārcus arborem nōn _____.
7. _____, cūr tū nōn arborem ascendis?
8. Dāvus est vir _____.
9. Puerī _____ rīdent.
10. Cornēlia et Flāvia sunt _____.
11. _____ servī in Italiā _____.

Rōmānus/Rōmāna ✓
currit/currunt
amīcus/amīcī ✓
servus/servī ✓
servus/servī ✓
ascendit/ascendunt
Mārcus/Mārce
Britannicus/Britannicī
laetus/laetī
dēfessa/dēfessae
Multī/Multae   labōrat/labōrant

BUILDING THE MEANING

Go Online
PHSchool.com
Web Code: jfd-0004

Direct Objects and the Ending -m

Look at these sentences taken from story 4:

        DO

Sextus <u>Cornēlia*m*</u> vexat. (4:1)   *Sextus annoys Cornelia.*

   DO

<u>Vōce*m*</u> Cornēlia audit. (4:3–4)   *Cornelia hears the voice.*

In these sentences, the words that end in *-m*, namely **Cornēlia*m*** and **vōce*m***, are said to be the *direct objects* (DO) of the verbs **vexat** and **audit**. They name the person or thing that receives the action of the verb.

In English, the order of the words in a sentence usually tells us what word is the direct object; the direct object usually follows the verb, e.g., Cornelia hears <u>the voice</u>. In Latin, it is the ending *-m* that indicates the direct object in the sentence **Vōce*m* Cornēlia audit.** The Latin words could be arranged in any order, and they would still convey essentially the same message.

Note that the pronouns **mē** and **tē**, seen in line 7 of the story on page 19, are also direct objects, although they do not have the ending *-m*.

Transitive and Intransitive Verbs

Verbs that take direct objects are said to be *transitive verbs* and may be labeled TV. Verbs that do not take direct objects are said to be *intransitive verbs* (IV), e.g., **Cornēlia sub arbore sedet,** *Cornelia sits under the tree* (1:3).

Core Elements of Latin Sentences

A complete sentence usually has at least a subject and a verb. If the verb is a linking verb, a complement will be needed to complete the sentence. If the verb is transitive, a direct object will be needed to complete the sentence.

You have now met three different kinds of Latin sentences, each with a different selection of core elements as follows:

1. Subject and Intransitive Verb:

     S   IV

    Sextus ex arbore cadit. (4:9)

2. Subject, Linking Verb, and Complement:

     S   LV   C   S   C   LV

    Sextus est puer molestus. (4:1)   Brevī tempore **Cornēlia dēfessa est.** (2:3–4)

3. Subject, Direct Object, and Transitive Verb:

     S   DO   TV   DO   S   TV

    Magna vōx Cornēliam terret. (4:4)   **Vōcem Cornēlia audit.** (4:3–4)

For a fuller discussion of the core elements of Latin sentences and for more examples, see pages 274–275, II.A, B, C, and D.

EXERCISE 4c

Read each sentence aloud, identify core elements, and translate:

1. Sextus Dāvum saepe vexat; Sextum Dāvus nōn amat.
2. Puellae Mārcum et servum cōnspiciunt.
3. Magna vōx puellam terret.
4. Magnam arborem Sextus ascendit.
5. Dāvus, quī fragōrem audit, est īrātus.

EXERCISE 4d

Using story 4 as a guide, give the Latin for:

1. Sextus is always annoying Cornelia.
2. Cornelia is tired and is sleeping under a tree.
3. Marcus runs to the tree and catches sight of the annoying boy.
4. Nothing frightens Sextus.
5. Marcus hears a big noise.

Romans and their style of painting can be remarkably modern looking, as in this artwork from Pompeii.

Word Study I

Latin and English

Over 60 percent of the words in the English language come from Latin. Look again at these words from Chapter 1:

pictūra   **habitat**

It is not difficult to think of English words that come from them:

picture   *inhabit*

The meanings and spellings of these English words show their relationship with Latin. Such words are called *derivatives*, since they are derived from (or come from) another language, in this case, Latin.

Of course, not all of English is derived from Latin. Most of the simple words of everyday English come from Anglo-Saxon, the Germanic ancestor of English. For this reason, many modern German words sound similar to English, such as "Buch" (*book*) and "Nacht" (*night*).

English words derived from Latin are usually the longer or more difficult words. For example, consider the two English words *water* and *aquatic*. The simpler word *water* is derived from the Anglo-Saxon "waeter" and is related to the German "Wasser." The more difficult word *aquatic* comes from the Latin word for water, **aqua**. Even if one did not know the meaning of *aquatic*, Latin would help to answer the following question:

Which of these is an aquatic sport?

(a) horseback riding   (c) swimming
(b) tennis   (d) soccer

Since *aquatic* means "related to water," the correct answer is "swimming." Knowledge of Latin will help with the meanings of over 60 percent of the words in the English language.

EXERCISE 1

Below are some Latin words from Chapters 1–4. Give the meaning of each word. Then, with the meaning in mind, think of at least one English word derived from each Latin word. Use each English word correctly in a sentence.

strēnua strength
multī multiple
sōlus solitary
nōmine nomenclature
servus servant

spectat spectacle
agrīs agriculture
terret terrefied
dēscende descend
vōx (vōce) voice

EXERCISE 2

Match each English word in the column at the left with its meaning in the column at the right. Use the meaning of the Latin word in parentheses as a guide.

1. *legible* (**legit**) I
2. *sedentary* (**sedet**) h
3. *ridicule* (**rīdet**) g
4. *virile* (**vir**) a
5. *elaborate* (**labōrat**) c
6. *audible* (**audit**) e
7. *conspicuous* (**cōnspicit**) b
8. *dormant* (**dormit**) f
9. *inscribe* (**scrībit**) d

a. manly
b. easy to catch sight of
c. to work out carefully
d. to carve letters on stone
e. able to be heard
f. asleep, inactive
g. to make fun of, mock
h. seated, stationary
i. able to be read

The Dictionary

An English dictionary is a useful source not only for finding the meanings of words but also for discovering the languages from which they are derived. Not all dictionaries provide information on derivation, but most larger ones do. In these more complete dictionaries, entries may include:

a. the word
b. a pronunciation guide
c. an abbreviation indicating the part of speech
d. derivation information
e. definition(s)

Locate these items of information in the following dictionary entry:

villain (vil´ ən), n. [O.Fr. *vilain* <L.L. *vīllānus* <L. *vīlla*, a country house]1. a wicked or evil person 2. a scoundrel.

This entry shows that the English word *villain* is a noun that comes from Old French "vilain," which is from the Late Latin **vīllānus**, which derives from Latin **vīlla**, meaning a country house. This derivation is especially interesting since it reveals the negative feelings toward country people that must have been prevalent at the time when the word *villain* came into use in English.

The abbreviations used in notes on derivation will be different from dictionary to dictionary. All abbreviations are explained at the beginning of each dictionary.

EXERCISE 3

Using a dictionary large enough to contain information on derivation, look up the following English words and copy down the complete derivation for each. Be prepared to explain these derivations as in the example above. All these English words are derived from Latin words you have met.

nominal   cadence   virtue   alter   ramify   infirm

MARCUS TO THE RESCUE

Cornēlia et Flāvia in hortō saepe ambulant. Sī diēs est calidus, ex hortō in silvam ambulant quod ibi est rīvus frīgidus. In eādem silvā puerī quoque saepe errant.

Hodiē, quod diēs est calidus, puellae sub arbore prope rīvum sedent. Dum ibi sedent, Flāvia, "Cūr Mārcus arborēs ascendere nōn vult? Estne puer ignāvus?" 5

"Minimē!" respondet Cornēlia. "Cūr tū Mārcum nōn amās? Mārcus neque ignāvus neque temerārius est."

Tum Flāvia, "Sed Mārcus est semper sollicitus. Sextum nihil terret."

Subitō lupum cōnspiciunt quī ad rīvum fūrtim dēscendit. Perterritae sunt puellae. Statim clāmant, "Mārce! Sexte! Ferte auxilium! Ferte auxilium!"

Puerī, ubi clāmōrem audiunt, statim ad puellās currunt. Lupus eōs iam cōnspicit. Tum Sextus, quod lupus eum terret, arborem petit et statim ascendit. Sed Mārcus rāmum arripit et lupum repellit. Puellae ē silvā currunt et ad vīllam salvae adveniunt. Brevī

(continued)

1 **sī,** conj., *if*
   diēs, *(a/the) day*
   calidus, *warm*
   in silvam, *into the woods*
2 **ibi,** adv., *there*
   rīvus, *(a/the) stream*
   frīgidus, *cool, cold*
3 **errant,** *(they) wander*
4 **prope,** *near*
5 **vult,** *(he/she) wishes, wants*
   ignāvus, *cowardly, lazy*
6 **respondet,** *(he/she) replies*
   neque...neque..., conj., *neither...nor...*
7 **temerārius,** *rash, reckless, bold*

9 **lupus,** *(a/the) wolf*
   perterritus, *frightened, terrified*
10 **statim,** adv., *immediately*
   Ferte auxilium! *Bring help! Help!*
11 **ubi,** conj., *where, when*
   clāmor, *(a/the) shout, shouting*
   ad puellās, *toward the girls*
   eōs, *them*
12 **eum,** *him*
   petit, *(he/she) looks for, seeks*
13 **arripit,** *(he/she) grabs hold of, snatches*
   repellit, *(he/she) drives off*
   ē silvā, *out of the woods*
   salvae, *safe*
   adveniunt, *(they) reach, arrive (at)*

EXERCISE 5a

Respondē Latīnē:

1. Ubi puellae hodiē sedent?
2. Cūr puellae perterritae sunt?
3. Quid faciunt puerī ubi clāmōrem audiunt?
4. Quem lupus terret?
   Quem...? *Whom...?*
5. Quid facit Mārcus?

Go Online
PHSchool.com
Web Code: jfd-0005

tempore, ubi Mārcus advenit, eum laetae excipiunt. Sextus, puer ignāvus, adhūc sedet in arbore perterritus. Ex arbore dēscendere timet.

14 **excipiunt,** *(they) welcome*
   adhūc, adv., *still*

15 **timet,** *(he/she) fears, is afraid*

Respondē Latīnē:

6. Quālis puer est Sextus?

7. Cūr Sextus ex arbore nōn dēscendit?

EXERCISE 5b

Review

Decide whether each sentence is missing a subject or a direct object. Select the correct form of the noun. Then read aloud and translate:

1. Hodiē Sextus _____ ascendit.
   arbor/arborem
2. Sextus _____ conspicit.
   Mārcus/Mārcum
3. Nihil _____ terret.
   Sextum/Sextus
4. _____ puellae cōnspiciunt.
   Lupus/Lupum

5. Puerī _____ audiunt.
   arbore/arborem
6. _____ lupus terret.
   Sextus/Sextum
7. Puellae _____ laetae excipiunt.
   Mārcus/Mārcum
8. Hodiē _____ puerī nōn vexant.
   Dāvus/Dāvum

BUILDING THE MEANING

The Complementary Infinitive

In the story at the beginning of this chapter, you have seen how the meanings of some verbs may be expanded or completed by forms called *infinitives.* The words **Sextus vult**, *Sextus wants*, do not form a complete thought because we do not know what Sextus wants or wants to do. We can complete the thought as follows:

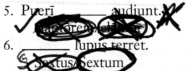

   Sextus arborem **ascendere** vult.   *Sextus wants to climb a/the tree.*

The meaning of the verb **vult** has now been completed with an infinitive **ascendere**, *to climb*, which itself takes the direct object **arborem**.

Here is another example:

   Sextus **dēscendere** timet.   *Sextus is afraid **to come down**.*

The infinitive is a form of a verb that can be recognized by the letters *-re* and is translated *to...*, e.g. **errāre**, *to wander*, **rīdēre**, *to laugh*, **ascendere**, *to climb*, and **dormīre**, *to sleep*.

Infinitives may be used to complete the meaning of verbs such as **vult**, *he/she wishes*, and **timet**, *he/she fears*, as in the sentences above, and of other verbs, some of which you will meet in Exercise 5c (see the list below the exercise).

When the infinitive is used in this way, it is called a *complementary infinitive* because it *completes* the meaning of the verb with which it goes. Note that in Latin a complementary infinitive usually comes *in front of* the verb, the meaning of which it completes, while in English it comes *after* the verb.

26   CHAPTER 5

EXERCISE 5c

Read aloud, identify infinitives, and translate:

1. Ego ad hortum currō quod Dāvum vexāre volō.
2. Ego arborem nōn ascendō quod in rīvum cadere nōlō.
3. Quod diēs est calidus, tū prope rīvum errāre parās.
4. Lupus ad vīllam fūrtim appropinquat; servus eum repellere nōn potest.
5. Sextus ex arbore dēscendere nōn vult quod lupus eum terret.
6. Ego magnam arborem ascendere timeō.
7. Lupus Sextum in arbore cōnspicere nōn potest.
8. Mārcus lupum cōnspicit, rāmum arripit, lupum repellere parat.
9. Sī diēs est calidus, Mārcus vult ambulāre in silvam ubi prope rīvum frīgidum sedēre potest.
10. In hortum exīre nōlō quod in vīllā labōrāre volō.

ego, *I*	**parās,** *you prepare, get ready*
volō, *I wish, want*	**potest,** *(he/she) is able, can*
nōlō, *I do not wish, want*	**exīre,** *to go out*

EXERCISE 5d

Using story 5 and Exercise 5c as guides, give the Latin for:

1. Cornelia often wishes to wander in the woods.
2. Flavia wishes to climb the large tree.
3. Marcus is able to drive off the wolf.
4. Sextus is afraid to come down out of the tree.
5. Sextus does not want to fall into the stream.

A confrontation between two of the most feared wild animals, a wolf and a bull, is depicted in this mosaic.
Mosaic, Rome

Myth I

CA. 1184 B.C.

Go Online
PHSchool.com
Web Code: jfd-0005

gentue case = ownership

AENEAS

The members of our Roman family are proud of their heritage, and take particular pride in the deeds accomplished by other Cornelii throughout the history of Rome. As a people, the Romans were also proud of their mythological heritage. They traced their origins to the great Trojan hero, Aeneas, son of the goddess Venus and the mortal Anchises. According to the myth, Aeneas lived over 1200 years before the time we are studying and fought in the Trojan War.

According to legend, the Trojan War began when Paris, the son of King Priam of Troy, abducted Helen, Queen of Sparta, from her home and brought her back to Troy. Helen's outraged husband Menelaus appealed for help to his brother Agamemnon, King of Mycenae, who was then High King of the Greeks. Agamemnon assembled a huge army with contingents drawn from all regions of Greece. Each part of this force was, in turn, led by a king or prince of a region. These were the mighty Homeric heroes, so called because their stories were told by, among others, the Greek poet Homer in his epic poems, the *Iliad* and the *Odyssey*. The Greek army contained the most famous heroes

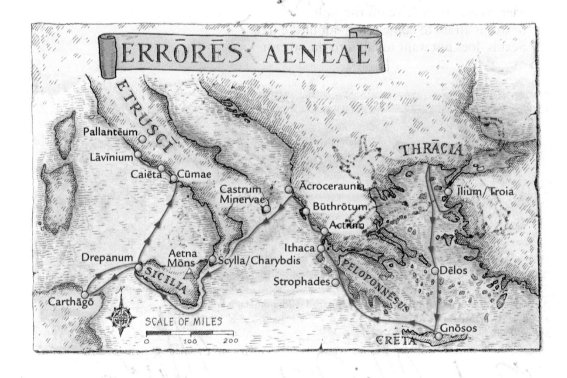

ERRŌRĒS · AENĒAE

Sinon explains to King Priam why the Greeks left the horse (*top*). The priest Laocoon thrusts his spear into the horse's side to protest accepting the Greek gift (*bottom*).
Episode of The Aeneid: *The Trojan Horse, painted enamel, ca. 1530–1540, Master of* The Aeneid *Series*

[handwritten notes in margins:]
Venus is the mother of Aneas
Trojan/Roman
omans
immortal
Venus — Mother of Aenenas
Achies — father of aenenas
Paris — son of priam
King Priam
Helen (wife of menelaus) Agamenma — King and brother of Melaus

of this age, including Ulysses (called Odysseus by the Greeks), the most cunning of the Greeks, and Achilles, the mightiest warrior. With this army Agamemnon set sail for Asia Minor and laid siege to the city of Troy.

The Trojans had their own heroes for defense, primarily the sons of King Priam; the greatest warrior among these was Hector, who commanded the Trojan army. Second to Hector in reputation was Aeneas, a Dardanian from the area north of the city. He had brought his own contingent of Dardanian troops to help in the defense and had moved into Troy with his men and his family early in the war. Powerful though the attacking Greek army was, it was unable to lay an effective siege around such a large city, and the Trojans were able to draw supplies and reinforcements from the surrounding countryside. The resulting stalemate lasted ten years, according to legend.

[handwritten notes in margins:]
The Greeks
Ulusses — A cunning fighter (thought of Trojan horse
Achilles — Strong fighter, big — Thought to be immortal accept one weakness was heal

In the tenth year of the war, after the deaths of many warriors on both sides, including Hector and Achilles, the Greeks finally managed to take the city, owing to a wily deception devised by Ulysses. The Greek army constructed a huge wooden horse, inside of which they hid Greek soldiers. They gave the horse to the Trojans on the pretext that it was a gift to appease the goddess Minerva, whom they had offended, and they pretended to depart the area in force. Actually, though, once the horse was inside the city, the Greek soldiers emerged from its belly and proceeded to lay waste Troy and its inhabitants. That night as the Trojans, caught utterly by surprise, tried desperately to defend their city, the gods themselves spoke to Aeneas. They told him that Troy was destined to fall and that he should not waste his life defending the city. Instead, they revealed that Aeneas's mission was to leave Troy and found a new city where a new nation could be

The arrival of Aeneas at Pallanteum, the future site of Rome
Landscape with the Arrival of Aeneas at Pallanteum, *detail, Claude Lorrain*

established, springing from Trojan stock. Aeneas hurriedly gathered his family and his men and left the city in the confusion of the Greek assault. Although his wife Creusa was tragically lost during the flight, Aeneas and twenty shiploads of companions, together with Anchises his father and Ascanius his son, successfully escaped the ruin of Troy.

Aeneas wandered the lands of the Mediterranean for many years, for although the gods had told him to found a new city, they had not told him where. After abortive attempts to settle in Thrace, on Crete, and at Carthage with Dido, an exiled Phoenician queen, Aeneas finally arrived at Italy where he was destined to found his city. That city was not actually Rome. It was Lavinium, named after Lavinia, the daughter of King Latinus, ruler of Latium, who became the wife of Aeneas. After the marriage of Aeneas and Lavinia, the name of Latins was bestowed upon their combined peoples, the Italians of the kingdom of Latium and the exiled Trojans resettling in the new land.

The story of Aeneas's wanderings from Troy, his many adventures in the waters and lands of the Mediterranean, his struggles and his loves, through to his arrival in Italy and the founding of his city in Latium, was told by the Roman poet Publius Vergilius Maro in his epic poem, the *Aeneid*.

The opening lines of that epic are:

> Of war and a man I sing, who first from Troy's shores, an exile by the decree of fate, came to Italy and Lavinium's shores. Much was he tossed on sea and land by the violence of the gods, because of cruel Juno's unforgetting anger. Much, too, did he endure in war as he sought to found a city and bring his gods to Latium. From him are descended the Latin people, the elders of Alba, and the walls of lofty Rome.

---

1. Why do you suppose the Romans traced their origins back to Aeneas and the Trojan War?
2. In the modern world, there is even a computer virus named after the mythical Trojan Horse. Why does this story have such staying power?

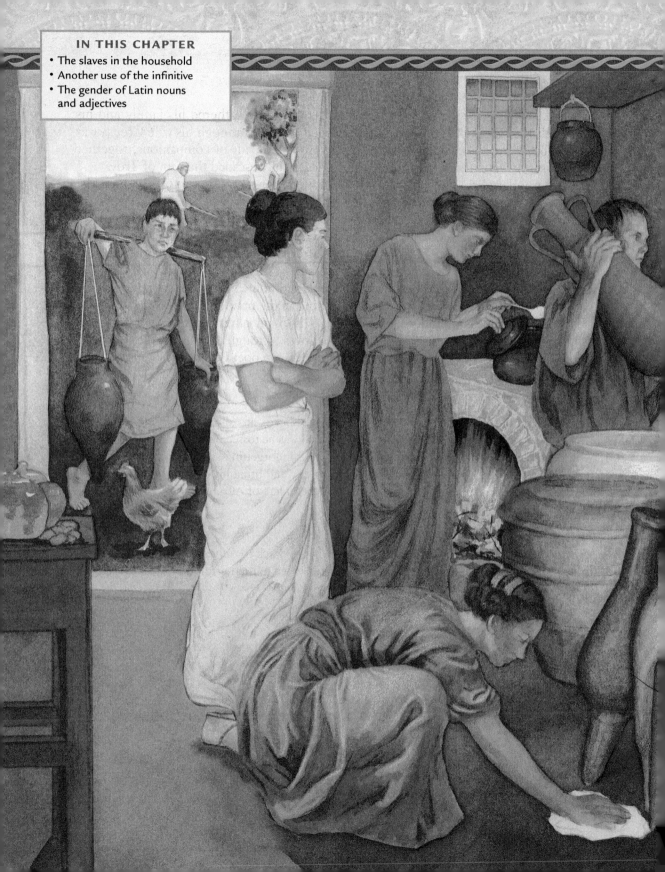

EARLY IN THE DAY

Nōndum lūcet, sed Cornēlia surgit et per vīllam ambulat. Adhūc dormiunt pater et māter et Mārcus. Etiam Sextus dormit neque Cornēliam vexat. Nōn tamen dormiunt servī et ancillae. Omnēs iam surgunt et labōrāre parant quod Cornēlium et Aurēliam timent.

Cornēlia ancillam, nōmine Syram, observat quae vīllam pūrgat et alteram, nōmine   5
Thressam, quae cibum coquere parat. Multī servī mox in agrōs currunt ubi strēnuē labōrant. Aquam ē rīvō in vīllam portant.

Iam surgunt Cornēlius et Aurēlia. Cornēlius petit Dāvum quī in hortō est. Īrātus subitō est Cornēlius. Dāvum reprehendit quod sub arbore sedet neque labōrat. Dāvus, ubi Cornēlium audit, statim surgit et labōrāre parat.   10

Aurēlia Cornēliam docet vīllam cūrāre. Ancillae vīllam pūrgant, cibum coquunt, lānam trahunt. Reprehendit Aurēlia ancillās sī ignāvae sunt. Mātrem observat Cornēlia et omnia quae māter facit facere parat. Mātrem adiuvāre vult, sed ipsa neque servum neque ancillam reprehendit. Servī et ancillae nunc strēnuē labōrant. Necesse est neque servum neque ancillam reprehendere.   15

1	**nōndum,** adv., *not yet*
	lūcet, *it is light, it is day*
	surgit, *(he/she) gets up, rises*
	per vīllam, *through the country house*
	pater, *father*
2	**māter,** *mother*
	etiam, adv., *also, even*
	neque, conj., *and...not*
	tamen, adv., *however*
3	**ancilla,** *slave-woman*
	omnēs, *all*
5	**observat,** *(he/she) watches*
	pūrgat, *(he/she) cleans*
6	**cibus,** *food*

	coquere, *to cook*
	mox, adv., *soon, presently*
	strēnuē, adv., *strenuously, hard*
7	**aqua,** *water*
	portant, *(they) carry*
9	**reprehendit,** *(he/she) blames, scolds*
11	**docet,** *(he/she) teaches*
	cūrāre, *to look after, take care of*
12	**lānam trahunt,** *(they) spin wool*
13	**omnia quae,** *everything that*
	adiuvāre, *to help*
	ipsa, *she herself*
14	**nunc,** adv., *now*
	necesse est, *it is necessary*

EXERCISE 6a

Respondē Latīnē:

1. Quis surgit?
2. Quī dormiunt?
3. Quid faciunt servī et ancillae?
4. Quid servī ē rīvō in vīllam portant?
   Quī...? *Who...?* (plural)

5. Cūr Cornēlius īrātus est?
6. Quid Aurēlia Cornēliam docet?
7. Quid Cornēlia facere parat?
8. Quid Cornēlia nōn facit?

Go Online
PHSchool.com
Web Code: jfd-0006

BUILDING THE MEANING

Infinitive with Impersonal Verbal Phrase

An infinitive usually occurs with the verbal phrase **necesse est**:

> Necesse est neque servum neque ancillam **reprehendere**. (6:14–15)
> *It is necessary* **to scold** *neither slave nor slave-woman.*

The verbal phrase **necesse est** is said to be *impersonal* because we supply the subject "it."

Nouns and Adjectives: Gender

The meaning of basic Latin sentences may be expanded by the addition of modifiers such as adjectives. Compare the following sets of sentences:

Mārcus est puer.	Cornēlia est puella.
Marcus is a boy.	*Cornelia is a girl.*
Mārcus est puer **Rōmānus**.	Cornēlia est puella **Rōmāna**.
*Marcus is a **Roman** boy.*	*Cornelia is a **Roman** girl.*

The adjectives **Rōmānus** and **Rōmāna** are said to *modify* the nouns that they describe, namely **puer** and **puella**. In order to understand the grammatical relationship between Latin adjectives and the nouns they modify, you need to know more about Latin nouns.

Latin nouns are said to have *gender*. We say that **Mārcus** and **puer** are *masculine* nouns and that **Cornēlia** and **puella** are *feminine* nouns.

Names of men and boys, such as **Cornēlius** and **Mārcus**, and words that designate men and boys, such as **vir** and **puer**, are masculine. Most nouns, such as **hortus**, that end in *-us* are also masculine, even those that do not refer to males.

Names of women and girls, such as **Aurēlia** and **Cornēlia**, and words that designate women and girls, such as **fēmina** and **puella**, are feminine. Most other nouns that end in *-a*, such as **vīlla** and **pictūra**, are also feminine, even those that do not refer to females.

EXERCISE 6b

Tell the gender of each noun below:

1. Aurēlia	4. amīcus	7. rāmus	10. Sextus
2. stola	5. piscīna	8. vir	11. servus
3. Dāvus	6. toga	9. amīca	12. palla

Note that in the following examples the adjective ends in *-us* when it modifies **Mārcus, puer,** and **vir** (masculine nouns) and that it ends in *-a* when it modifies **puella** (feminine):

Mārcus est **Rōmānus**.	Cornēlius est vir **Rōmānus**.
Mārcus est puer **Rōmānus**.	Cornēlia est puella **Rōmāna**.

The endings of both nouns and adjectives change when they become direct objects or become plural:

Masculine	Feminine
Subject or complement singular:	
serv***us*** Britannic***us***	puell***a*** laet***a***
Object singular:	
serv***um*** Britannic***um***	puell***am*** laet***am***
Subject or complement plural:	
serv***ī*** Britannic***ī***	puell***ae*** laet***ae***

The gender of many nouns is not so easy to predict, but you can tell by looking at an adjective used to describe the noun:

Magn*us* <u>clāmor</u> in hortō est.
*There is **great** <u>shouting</u> in the garden.*

<u>Arbor</u> est **magn*a***.
*The <u>tree</u> is **big**.*

<u>Diēs</u> est **calid*us***.
*The <u>day</u> is **hot**.*

The **-*us*** on **magnus** shows that **clāmor** is masculine, the **-*a*** on **magna** shows that **arbor** is feminine, and the **-*us*** on **calidus** shows that **diēs** is masculine.

EXERCISE 6c

Read each sentence aloud. In each sentence identify the adjective and the noun that it modifies or describes. Use the ending on the adjective to determine whether the noun it modifies or describes is masculine or feminine. Then translate the sentence:

1. Cornēlia magnum fragōrem audit.
2. Puerī sunt laetī.
3. Puella sollicita magnam vōcem audit.
4. Magnum clāmōrem nōn amat Dāvus.
5. Sextus est puer strēnuus.
6. Dāvus puerum strēnuum nōn amat.
7. Puerī ad vīllam vīcīnam currunt.
8. Dāvus nōn est Rōmānus.
9. Puellae laetae in agrīs errant.
10. Magnam arborem puerī in agrīs vident.

EXERCISE 6d

Using story 6 as a guide, give the Latin for:

1. Marcus is sleeping because he is tired.
2. The energetic slaves are not sleeping.
3. Cornelius scolds lazy Davus.
4. Many slaves carry cold water.
5. Aurelia scolds a lazy slave-woman.

Romans prized creatively designed glassware, such as this jug.
Second to third century A.D.

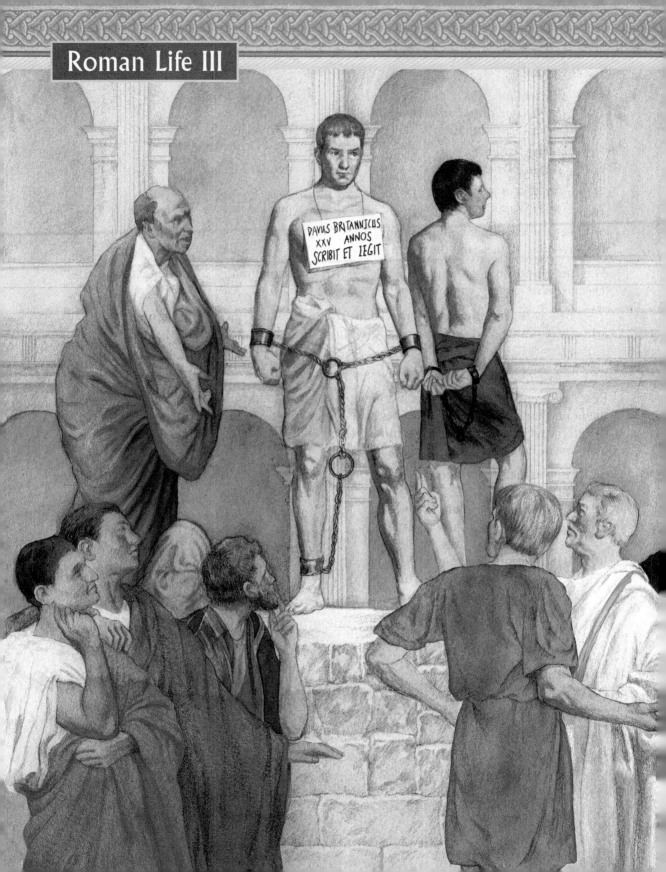

THE SLAVE MARKET

Slaves, who were in the early days mainly prisoners of war, were plentiful, and even the poorest Roman household might own one or two. Davus had been captured in Britain and sent to Rome to be sold by auction in the Forum. When his feet were whitened with chalk by the slave-dealer, Davus was mystified, but he soon discovered that this had been done to all new arrivals from abroad. A placard was hung around his neck indicating that he was British and could read and write. He was then put on a revolving stand, and bidding for him began.

He felt pretty uncomfortable standing there like an exhibit at the cattle-market, but he put the best face on it, looking around challengingly at the bidders. Titus Cornelius, father of Gaius Cornelius, was in the Forum that day with the overseer (**vīlicus**) of his farm to purchase some new slaves. He did not pay much attention to the placard—**mangōnēs**, as slave-dealers were called, were notorious swindlers—but when he saw Davus's fine physique, fair hair, and blue eyes he made a bid of 5,000 sesterces, and Davus soon found himself beside the overseer and his new master.

By this time Titus was offering 10,000 sesterces for a Greek from Rhodes. This puzzled Davus because the fellow was a pale, half-starved individual who looked as if a hard day's work would kill him. The overseer, too, looked annoyed at this extravagant bid but said nothing. But when he heard Titus being forced up to 20,000, then 30,000, he could contain himself no longer and muttered angrily, "He's not worth half that, master!" But Titus ignored him and finally paid 35,000 for the Greek Eucleides. The odd qualifications on the placard, "skilled in geometry and rhetoric," must, the overseer thought, have had something to do with the record price!

As Davus, along with the strange Greek, was packed on a cart with some tough-looking Thracians also bought that day, he was filled with fear and doubt as to what might happen to him. But he needn't have worried. Old Titus proved to be the kindest of masters, and now, thirty years later, Davus, himself a grizzled fifty-five, was overseer of the farm. On some of the neighboring estates, he knew, things were not so good.

NEWS FROM ROME

In vīllā sedet vir Rōmānus, nōmine Gāius Cornēlius, quī est pater Mārcī et Cornēliae. Cornēlius est senātor Rōmānus. Sōlus sedet quod multās epistulās scrībere vult. Dum pater occupātus est, Mārcus et Sextus et Cornēlia in agrīs vīcīnīs errant. Ibi multōs servōs labōrantēs spectant.

Subitō nūntium cōnspiciunt quī ad eōs venit. Nūntius, ubi advenit, puerōs salūtat.   5
"Salvē!" respondet Mārcus. "Quem tū petis?"
Nūntius, "Gāium Cornēlium petō," inquit.
Mārcus, "Gāius Cornēlius est pater meus," inquit. "Est in vīllā." Nūntium in vīllam dūcit et patrem petit.
"Pater," inquit Mārcus, "nūntius in vīllā est."   10
Cornēlius statim venit et nūntium salūtat. Epistulam nūntius trādit. Cornēlius, ubi epistulam legit, "Ēheu!" inquit. "Prīnceps senātōrēs Rōmānōs ad urbem revocat. Eōs cōnsulere vult. Necesse est ad urbem redīre."
"Eugepae!" clāmat Sextus, quī Rōmam īre vult. Gemit Cornēlia quod Flāvia ad urbem venīre nōn potest.   15

occupātus, *busy*
4 **labōrantēs,** *working*
spectant, *(they) watch, look at*
5 **nūntius,** *messenger*
venit, *(he/she) comes*
salūtat, *(he/she) greets*
6 **Salvē!** *Greetings! Hello!*
7 **inquit,** *(he/she) says*
8 **meus,** *my*
dūcit, *(he/she) leads, takes*

trādit, *(he/she) hands over*
12 **Ēheu!** interj., *Alas! Oh no!*
prīnceps, *emperor*
ad urbem, *to the city*
revocat, *(he/she) recalls*
13 **cōnsulere,** *to consult*
redīre, *to return*
14 **Eugepae!** interj., *Hurray!*
īre, *to go*

Epistulas—letters

EXERCISE 7a

Respondē Latīnē:

1. Cūr Cornēlius sōlus sedet?
2. Ubi Mārcus et Sextus et Cornēlia errant?
3. Quōs spectant in agrīs?   **Quōs...?** *Whom...?* (plural)
4. Quis advenit?
5. Quem nūntius petit?
6. Cūr prīnceps senātōrēs Rōmānōs ad urbem revocat?
7. Quis clāmat "Eugepae!"? Cūr?
8. Cūr gemit Cornēlia?

Go Online
PHSchool.com
Web Code: jfd-0007

Nouns and Adjectives:
The Endings -ās, -ōs, and -ēs

Look at these three sentences:

Mult**ās** epistul**ās** scrībit.	*He writes many letters.*
Mult**ōs** serv**ōs** spectant.	*They watch many slaves.*
Senātōr**ēs** Rōmān**ōs** revocat.	*He recalls the Roman senators.*

The words **multās epistulās, multōs servōs,** and **senātōrēs Rōmānōs** introduce you to new endings. You already know that most singular Latin nouns and adjectives end in *-m* when they are used as direct objects (DO) (see page 20). Plural nouns and adjectives used as direct objects usually end in *-s* preceded by a long vowel, e.g., **multās epistulās, multōs servōs,** and **senātōrēs Rōmānōs.**

EXERCISE 7b

Read each sentence aloud. Then locate the direct object in each sentence and say whether it is singular or plural. Also locate any adjectives, identify the nouns that they modify, and give the gender of each of these nouns. Then translate:

1. Cornēlius multās epistulās scrībit.
2. Puerī magnam arborem in agrīs vident.
3. Nūntius quī ad puerōs venit magnōs clāmōrēs audit.
4. Magnās vōcēs audit.
5. Nūntius puerōs dēfessōs salūtat.
6. Prīnceps senātōrēs Rōmānōs ad urbem revocat.
7. Sextus ad magnam urbem īre vult.
8. Cornēlia ad urbem redīre nōn vult quod vīllam rūsticam et amīcam vīcīnam amat.

EXERCISE 7c

Using story 7 as a guide, give the Latin for:

1. Cornelius wants to write many letters.
2. Marcus and Sextus watch many slaves working in the fields.
3. The messenger greets the boys.
4. The messenger is looking for Gaius Cornelius.
5. The messenger hands over a letter.
6. It is necessary to return to the city immediately.
7. Sextus wishes to go to Rome, but Flavia cannot.

Roman writing artifacts

Nouns: Cases and Declensions

Nominative and Accusative Cases

The form of the Latin noun when used as the *subject* of a verb or as a *complement* with **est** or **sunt** is known as the *nominative case*.

The form of the Latin noun when used as the *direct object* of a verb is known as the *accusative case*.

For example:

Nominative	Accusative
Lup**us** eum terret.	Puellae lup**um** vident.
The wolf frightens him.	*The girls see the wolf.*
Lup**ī** puerōs terrent.	Servī lup**ōs** repellunt.
The wolves frighten the boys.	*The slaves drive off the wolves.*
Puell**a** est laet**a**.	Māter puell**am** laet**am** videt.
The girl is happy.	*The mother sees the happy girl.*

— Memorize

Most nouns that you have met belong in the following groups or *declensions:*

Number Case	1st Declension	2nd Declension			3rd Declension	
Singular						
Nominative	puéll**a**	sérv**us**	púer	áger	páter	vōx
Accusative	puéll**am**	sérv**um**	púer**um**	ágr**um**	pátr**em**	vṓc**em**
Plural						
Nominative	puéll**ae**	sérv**ī**	púer**ī**	ágr**ī**	pátr**ēs**	vṓc**ēs**
Accusative	puéll**ās**	sérv**ōs**	púer**ōs**	ágr**ōs**	pátr**ēs**	vṓc**ēs**

Be sure to learn these forms thoroughly. Note how each word is accented.

NOTES

1. In the 2nd declension, most nouns end in *-us* in the nominative singular (e.g., **servus**), but there are a few like **puer, ager,** and **vir** that end in *-r*. In both types, however, the accusative singular ends in *-um* and the accusative plural in *-ōs*.
2. Although **arbor, pater,** and **māter** end in *-r*, their other endings identify them as 3rd declension nouns.
3. In the 3rd declension, you will note that the nouns you have met end in different ways in the nominative singular (e.g., **arbor, prīnceps, urbs, pater, vōx**). Nevertheless, their accusative singulars all end in *-em*, and both nominative and accusative plurals end in *-ēs*.
4. Most 1st declension nouns are feminine; most 2nd declension nouns are masculine; some 3rd declension nouns are masculine, e.g., **pater**, and some are feminine, e.g., **vōx**.

EXERCISE 7d

In the sentences in Exercise 7b, locate all the nouns and identify their declension, gender, case, and number.

Reading with Attention to Cases

When you are reading a Latin sentence, identifying the case of each noun *as you meet it* will help you decide what the function of the word will be in the sentence as a whole. As you meet each noun and decide its function, you will form expectations about what is likely to come later to complete the meaning of the sentence.

Consider the following sentences:

1. **Servus currit.**
   The first word we meet is **servus**. We know that it is the subject of the verb because we recognize that it is in the nominative case. The verb (**currit**) then tells us what the slave is "doing."

2. **Servus Dāvum cōnspicit.**
   We go from **servus** (nominative = subject) to **Dāvum** and recognize that **Dāvum** is the direct object of the verb because we recognize it as accusative case. **Dāvum** also tells us that the verb in this sentence is transitive, because **Dāvum** is a direct object and direct objects appear only with transitive verbs. The verb tells us what the slave is "doing" to Davus.

3. **Dāvum puerī vexant.**
   The first word we meet is **Dāvum**. We recognize it as accusative case. The next word is **puerī**. We recognize that it is nominative, and therefore it is *the boys* who are doing something to Davus. The verb **vexant** tells us what they are doing.

4. **Rāmum arripit.**
   We recognize **Rāmum** as accusative case, and we know immediately that someone is doing something to a branch. Since there is no noun in the nominative case, the *ending* of the verb indicates the subject (*he/she*) and the *meaning* of the verb completes the sense.

EXERCISE 7e

Read each sentence aloud. Identify subjects and direct objects, as in the examples above. Then translate:

1. Lupus puellās terret. *The wolf scares the girls*
2. Puellae silvam amant. *the Girs love the woods*
3. Dāvum et servōs puerī vexāre nōn timent. *the wolves often scare*
4. Puerōs et puellās lupī semper terrent.
5. Servī lupōs ex agrīs repellunt. *the slave drive the wolves Out of the fields*

3. the boys are not affraid to scare davus and the servant

Mercury, the Roman god of messengers. The wings on the head and feet and the caduceus, or herald's wand, identify this figure as Mercury.
Detail of the ceiling of Palazzo Clerici, Milan, Italy

Nominative or Accusative Plural?
How Do You Decide?

In 3rd declension nouns, the ending of both the nominative and accusative plural is *-ēs*. When you meet a noun with this ending, you cannot tell from the word itself whether it will be a subject or a direct object. To do so in the sentences below, you must first identify the case of the other noun in each sentence. Note the kind of logic modeled below these sentences:

1. Puerī clāmōrēs audiunt.
2. Puerōs clāmōrēs terrent.
3. Prīnceps senātōrēs excipit.
4. Prīncipem senātōrēs excipiunt.
5. Clāmōrēs mātrēs audiunt.
6. Magnōs clāmōrēs patrēs audiunt.
7. Magnī clāmōrēs patrēs terrent.

In sentence 1, since **puerī** is in the nominative case and is therefore the subject of the verb, **clāmōrēs** must be in the accusative case and is therefore the direct object.

In sentence 2, since **puerōs** is accusative, **clāmōrēs** must be nominative.

In sentence 3, since **prīnceps** is nominative, we assume that **senātōrēs** will be accusative. This is confirmed by the singular transitive verb **excipit**.

In sentence 4, since **prīncipem** is accusative, we assume that **senātōrēs** will be nominative. This is confirmed by the fact that the verb **excipiunt** is plural.

In sentence 5, where both nouns end in *-ēs* and the verb is plural, it is the sense that indicates that **clāmōrēs** is accusative and **mātrēs** nominative.

In sentences 6 and 7 the endings on the adjectives tell that **clāmōrēs** is accusative in 6 and nominative in 7.

Read each sentence aloud. Identify subjects and direct objects, as in the preceding examples. Then translate:

1. Servus senātōrēs videt.
2. Arborēs puerī saepe ascendunt.
3. Clāmōrēs puellās terrent.
4. Patrēs magnōs fragōrēs audiunt.
5. Patrem vōcēs vexant.
6. Vōcēs in hortō audit.
7. Patrēs in viā cōnspiciunt.
8. Patrēs puerōs in viā cōnspiciunt.
9. Patrēs sollicitī clāmōrēs audiunt.
10. Magnās vōcēs patrēs audiunt.

Peristyle of the luxurious *vīlla urbāna* owned by Poppaea Sabina, wife of the emperor Nero, at Oplontis, between Pompeii and Herculaneum
Torre Annunziata, Italy, first century A.D.

ADDITIONAL READING:
The Romans Speak for Themselves: Book I: "Roman Roots in the Country," pages 10–17.

THE ROMAN VILLA

I n cities, the majority of Romans lived in apartment buildings called **īnsulae**, which were several stories high. Cornelius, however, being a wealthy Roman, owned a self-contained house called a **domus**. We shall learn more about these town houses when Cornelius and his family reach Rome.

Like other rich Romans, Cornelius also had a house in the country. Roman country houses often had three distinct areas, each serving a different purpose. One area provided accommodation for the owner and his family when they came to the country from Rome, which they would usually do during the summer months to escape the noisy bustle and heat of the city. This area would include a garden with a fishpond, a dining room, bedrooms, a bakery, a tool room, baths, and a kitchen (see the ground plan on the next page, numbers 1–8). The second area housed the livestock and had quarters for the slaves, who lived on the estate year round and did the agricultural work (ground plan, numbers 9 and 12). The third area contained a room for pressing grapes, olive-pressing rooms, a farmyard with wine vats, a barn for storing grain, and an open space (**ārea**) for threshing grain (ground plan, numbers 10 and 13–16). All three areas taken together could be referred to as a **vīlla rūstica**.

When absent, Cornelius placed the day-to-day running of the **vīlla rūstica** in the capable hands of Davus, his overseer (**vīlicus**), but some landowners had tenant farmers. Roman writers on agriculture stress that the owner should take special care in the selection of his farm staff and in the working relationships between himself and his staff:

> The owner should conduct himself civilly with his tenants, and speak affably, not haughtily, to them; he should be more concerned about their work than their payments of rent, because this offends them less and in the long run is more profitable. For the position of **vīlicus,** a man should be chosen who has borne up under heavy work, one who has been tried by experience. He should be past young manhood and yet not be old, because older men think it beneath them to take orders from a young man, and an old man will break down under heavy labor. Let him be middle-aged, strong, skilled in farming or at least able to learn. As for the other slaves, I myself talk rather familiarly with them for it lightens their toil, and I even make jokes with them and allow them to make jokes. I also now make it my practice to consult them on any new work, as if they were experienced, so that I can come to know their abilities. Moreover, they are more willing to undertake a task on which they think their opinions have been asked and on which I have followed their advice.

Columella, *On Agriculture* I. VII–VIII (extracts)

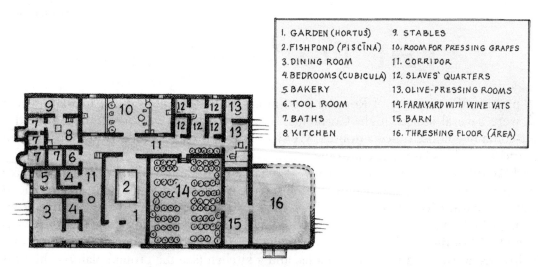

1. GARDEN (HORTUS)	9. STABLES
2. FISHPOND (PISCĪNA)	10. ROOM FOR PRESSING GRAPES
3. DINING ROOM	11. CORRIDOR
4. BEDROOMS (CUBICULA)	12. SLAVES' QUARTERS
5. BAKERY	13. OLIVE-PRESSING ROOMS
6. TOOL ROOM	14. FARMYARD WITH WINE VATS
7. BATHS	15. BARN
8. KITCHEN	16. THRESHING FLOOR (ĀREA)

GROUND PLAN OF *Vīlla Rūstica* OF THE *Cornēliī*

Reconstructed View of the
Vīlla Rūstica of the *Cornēliī*

ADDITIONAL READING:
The Romans Speak for Themselves: Book I: "Pliny's Laurentine Villa," pages 18–26, and
"A Pleasant Retreat," pages 27–32.

If Cornelius had been a very wealthy Roman, he might have had a **vīlla urbāna**, literally a "city villa," separate from the accommodations for the farm. Such a **vīlla urbāna** could be very luxurious and could take up almost the whole estate. It could have winter and summer apartments oriented to the seasonal sunlight, baths, and promenades, just like a house in the city. The Roman author Pliny the Younger describes his **vīlla urbāna** near Laurentum in a letter to a friend. Below is a ground plan of his country house. Such country houses by the sea (**mare**) were also called **vīllae maritimae**. These luxury houses offered their owners all the comforts of a city house in the beauty and quiet of the country.

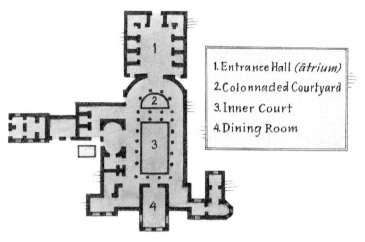

1. Entrance Hall (*ātrium*)
2. Colonnaded Courtyard
3. Inner Court
4. Dining Room

PLAN OF PLINY THE YOUNGER'S
VĪLLA URBĀNA

The Romans loved natural beauty and artistic representations of it. They often had the walls of their houses (in both the city and the country) painted, as Pliny the Younger's uncle, Pliny the Elder, describes them, with pictures "of country houses and landscaped gardens, copses, woods, hills, fish ponds and canals, rivers, coasts, and any other scenery one could desire, and scenes of people strolling along or sailing in a boat, or traveling to the country in carriages, people fishing, fowling and hunting, or gathering grapes" (Pliny the Elder, *Natural History* 35.116).

Pliny the Younger had another **vīlla urbāna** in Etruria with luxurious fountains, pools, and baths, which he describes as follows:

> Opposite the dining room at the corner of the colonnade is a large bedroom. From some of its windows you look onto the terrace, from others onto the meadow, while the windows in front overlook an ornamental pool which is a pleasure both to see and hear. For the water, falling from a height, foams white

in the marble basin. The bedroom is very warm in winter, being so exposed to the sun, and on a cloudy day the hot air from the nearby furnace takes the place of the sun's heat. From here you pass through a spacious and pleasant changing-room into the "cold bath" room in which there is a large bath out of the full sunlight. But if you want more space to swim in and warmer water, there is a pool in the courtyard and near it a fountain in which you can cool yourself if you've had enough of the heat.

And later in the same letter he tells us why he liked this house so much:

I can relax there with fuller and more carefree enjoyment. I need never wear a toga; nobody calls from next door. All is calm and quiet, which makes the place healthy, as do the clear sky and pure air. There I enjoy health of body and mind, for I keep my mind in training by study and my body by hunting.

Pliny the Younger, *Letters* V.6

1. What three areas make up the **vīlla rūstica**, and what function does each serve?
2. What would Titus Cornelius have been looking for if he had intended to purchase Davus to serve as the **vīlicus** of his estate?
3. Do you find Columella's advice on the treatment of slaves sound? Why or why not?

Wall painting adorning a bedroom of the *vīlla rūstica* of P. Fannius Synistor at Boscoreale near Pompeii. The painting shows an imaginary cityscape. The ground plan and a reconstruction of this villa are shown on page 46. We use this villa at Boscoreale as a model for the villa of the Cornelii at Baiae.
Boscoreale, Pompeii, first century A.D.

Review I: Chapters 1–7

Exercise Ia: The Elements of Sentences pp. 4, 8–9, 20–21, 26–27, 42

In the following sentences from the story in Chapter 7, identify each

subject

intransitive verb

linking verb

complement

transitive verb

direct object

complementary infinitive

1. In vīllā sedet vir Rōmānus.
2. Cornēlius est senātor Rōmānus.
3. Multās epistulās scrībere vult.
4. Dum pater occupātus est, Mārcus et Sextus et Cornēlia in agrīs errant.
5. Ibi multōs servōs labōrantēs spectant.
6. Flāvia ad urbem venīre nōn potest.

Exercise Ib: Nominative and Accusative pp. 40–43

Identify the declension of each noun. Then change nominatives to accusatives and accusatives to nominatives, keeping the same number (singular or plural):

1. cibus
2. lānam
3. fragōrem
4. aquae
5. lupus
6. virum
7. rīvī
8. vōcem
9. puerōs
10. patrem
11. rāmī
12. clāmōrēs

Exercise Ic: Agreement of Adjectives with Nouns pp. 14, 34–35

Select the appropriate adjective from the pool below to complete each of the following sentences. You may use adjectives more than once. Be sure to use the right ending on the adjective. Translate each sentence:

1. Dāvus _____ est quod puerī clāmant.
2. Sextus arborem ascendit quod _____ est.
3. Flāvia in vīllā _____ habitat.
4. Mārcus _____ rāmum arripit et lupum repellit.
5. Sextus _____ arborem ascendit.
6. Dāvus _____ est quod Sextus in hortō ambulat.
7. Flāvia et Cornēlia puellae _____ sunt et saepe in agrīs currunt.
8. Sextus est puer _____ et puellās terret.
9. Ubi lupus venit, Sextus in arbore sedet, quod puer _____ est.
10. Cornēlius _____ sedet quod epistulās scrībere vult.

sollicitus	vīcīnus	temerārius	strēnuus	ignāvus
sōlus	īrātus	molestus	magnus	

Exercise Id: Reading Comprehension

Read the following passage and answer the questions that follow with full sentences in Latin:

AENEAS LEAVES TROY

Aenēās est vir Troiānus quī urbem Troiam contrā Graecōs dēfendit. Decem annōs Graecī urbem obsident. Decem annōs Troiānī Graecōs repellunt. Tandem per dolum Graecī urbem nocte intrant. Multōs Troiānōs capiunt, multōs necant. Nōn iam urbem dēfendere Aenēās potest. Necesse est igitur ex urbe effugere et urbem novam petere. Multī amīcī quoque ab urbe Troiā effugiunt. 5 Omnēs ad Italiam nāvigāre parant.

Aenēās, dum ex urbe effugit, senem portat. Senex est Anchīsēs, pater Aenēae. Portāre Anchīsēn necesse est quod senex ambulāre nōn potest. Aenēās Anchīsēn portat; portat Anchīsēs Penātēs, deōs familiārēs. Deī Aenēān et Anchīsēn et omnēs amīcōs servant. 10

Aenēās etiam parvum puerum dūcit. Puer est Ascanius, fīlius Aenēae. Dum ex urbe ambulant, Ascanius patrem spectat et manum tenet. Perterritus est Ascanius quod magnōs clāmōrēs, magnōs fragōrēs audit. Valdē Graecōs timet.

Ubi Aenēās et Anchīsēs et Ascanius ex urbe effugiunt, "Ubi est māter?" subitō clāmat Ascanius. Multī amīcī adveniunt, sed nōn advenit Creūsa, māter 15 Ascaniī. Aenēās sollicitus patrem et fīlium et Penātēs relinquit et in urbem redit. Graecī ubīque sunt. Creūsam frūstrā petit.

"Ēheu!" inquit. "Troiam habent Graecī. Fortasse tē quoque habent, Creūsa. Valdē amō Creūsam, valdē Troiam. Sed neque urbem neque Creūsam servāre iam possum. Ad amīcōs igitur redīre necesse est." 20

Tum ad amīcōs redit. Mox ad Italiam nāvigāre parant Aenēās et amīcī.

1 Aenēās: Greek nominative	9 deōs familiārēs, *household gods*
contrā Graecōs, *against the Greeks*	deī, *the gods*
2 decem annōs, *for ten years*	Aenēān: Greek accusative
obsident, *(they) besiege*	10 servant, *(they) protect*
3 per dolum, *through a trick*	11 parvus, *small*
nocte, *at night*	fīlius, *son*
intrant, *(they) enter, go into*	12 manum, *hand*
capiunt, *(they) capture*	tenet, *(he/she) holds*
4 necant, *(they) kill*	13 valdē, *very much*
5 effugere, *to flee, run away, escape*	16 Ascaniī, *of Ascanius*
novus, *new*	relinquit, *(he/she) leaves*
ab urbe, *from the city*	17 ubīque, *everywhere*
6 nāvigāre, *to sail*	frūstrā, *in vain*
7 senem, *old man*	18 habent, *(they) have, hold*
Aenēae, *of Aeneas*	fortasse, *perhaps*
8 Anchīsēn: Greek accusative	19 servāre, *to save*
	20 possum, *I am able*

1. Who is Aeneas?
2. What do the Greeks do for ten years?
3. How do the Greeks finally enter the city?
4. Why is it necessary for Aeneas to flee?
5. What does Aeneas prepare to do?
6. Whom is Aeneas carrying?
7. What is Anchises carrying?
8. Whom is Aeneas leading?
9. Why is Ascanius frightened?
10. Who is Creusa?
11. Who goes back into the city?
12. Whom does he seek?
13. Is Aeneas able to save Creusa?
14. To where do Aeneas and his friends prepare to sail?

Aeneas carrying his father, Anchises, from the sack of Troy
The Flight of Aeneas from Troy, *1729, Carle van Loo*

GETTING UP EARLY

Nōndum lūcet, sed Aurēlia, māter Mārcī et Cornēliae, iam in vīllā occupāta est. Īrāta est quod servōs sedentēs cōnspicit.

"Agite, molestī servī!" inquit. "Cūr nihil facitis? Cūr vōs ibi sedētis? Cūr nōn strēnuē labōrātis? Omnia statim parāre necesse est quod nōs hodiē Rōmam redīmus." Iam strēnuē labōrant servī.   5

Tum Aurēlia puerōs excitāre parat. Intrat igitur cubiculum Mārcī. Clāmat, "Age, Mārce! Tempus est surgere. Nōs ad urbem redīre parāmus."

→Mārcus mātrem audit sed nihil respondet. Deinde Aurēlia cubiculum Sextī intrat. Clāmat, "Age, Sexte! Tempus est surgere." Statim surgit Sextus. Celeriter tunicam et togam induit et brevī tempore ē cubiculō currit.   left off here   10

→Iterum Aurēlia cubiculum Mārcī intrat. Iterum clāmat, "Age, Mārce! Nōs iam strēnuē labōrāmus. Cūr tū sōlus nōn surgis?"

Gemit Mārcus. "Ego nōn surgō," inquit, "quod Rōmam redīre nōlō. Cūr mihi quoque necesse est ad urbem redīre? Patrem meum prīnceps ad urbem revocat. Patrem cōnsulere vult. Nōn vult cōnsulere Mārcum."   15

Subitō intrat Gāius, pater Mārcī, et clāmat, "Sed ego volō cōnsulere Mārcum! Cūr, Mārce, hodiē mē vexās? Cūr nōn surgis? Cūr nōndum tunicam et togam induis, moleste puer?"

Nihil respondet Mārcus sed statim surgit quod patrem timet.

1 **iam,** adv., *now, already*
3 **Age!/Agite!** *Come on!*
  vōs, *you* (plural)
4 **nōs,** *we, us*
6 **excitāre,** *to rouse, wake (someone) up*
  intrat, *(he/she) enters*
  cubiculum, *room, bedroom*

7 **tempus,** *time*
8 **deinde,** adv., *then, next*
9 **celeriter,** adv., *quickly*
10 **induit,** *(he/she) puts on*
11 **iterum,** adv., *again, a second time*
13 **mihi,** *for me*

EXERCISE 8a

Respondē Latīnē:

1. Cūr est Aurēlia īrāta?
2. Cūr necesse est omnia statim parāre?
3. Quid Aurēlia in cubiculō Mārcī clāmat?
4. Quid facit Mārcus?

5. Surgitne Sextus?
6. Quid facit Sextus?
7. Cūr Mārcus nōn surgit?
8. Quis subitō intrat?
9. Cūr Mārcus surgit?

Go Online
PHSchool.com
Web Code: jfd-0008

Web Code: jfd-0008

Verbs: Persons

Look at these sentences:

Rōmam redīre nōl**ō**.	*I do not want to return to Rome.*
Cūr nōn surgi**s**?	*Why do **you** not get up?*
Aurēlia cubiculum Mārcī intra**t**.	***Aurelia** goes into Marcus's bedroom.*
Iterum clāma**t**.	***She** calls again.*
Ad urbem redīre parā**mus**.	***We** are preparing to return to the city.*
Cūr nōn strēnuē labōrā**tis**?	*Why do **you** not work hard?*
Puerī in agrīs erra**nt**. Servōs	*The **boys** wander in the fields.*
labōrantēs specta**nt**.	***They** watch the slaves working.*

The ending of the verb tells us who is doing something, i.e., whether the subject is 1st, 2nd, or 3rd *person, singular* or *plural* (I, you, he/she/it; we, you, they). In the 3rd person the subject may be a noun (e.g., **Aurēlia** and **puerī**). The 1st person is the speaker or speakers (I, we); the 2nd person is the person or persons spoken to (you, singular or plural); and the 3rd person is the person or thing or persons or things spoken about (he, she, it, they). The personal pronouns **ego, tū, nōs,** and **vōs** are used only for emphasis.

Person	Singular		Plural	
1	*-ō*	*I*	*-mus*	*we*
2	*-s*	*you*	*-tis*	*you*
3	*-t*	*he/she/it*	*-nt*	*they*

These personal endings always have the same meaning wherever they occur.

Person	Singular		Plural	
1	párō	*I prepare*	parámus	*we prepare*
2	párās	*you prepare*	parátis	*you prepare*
3	párat	*he/she prepares*	párant	*they prepare*

Be sure to learn these forms thoroughly.

Note that the vowel that precedes the personal endings is short before final *-t* and *-nt*. Note how each word is accented.

The following verb is irregular, but it uses the same endings as above (except for *-m* in place of *-ō* in the 1st person singular).

Person	Singular		Plural	
1	su**m**	*I am*	sú**mus**	*we are*
2	e**s**	*you are*	és**tis**	*you are*
3	es**t**	*he/she/it is*	su**nt**	*they are*

Be sure to learn these forms thoroughly.

EXERCISE 8b

Take parts and read these dialogues
aloud several times:

1. NĀRRĀTOR: Sextus est laetus.
   MĀRCUS: Tū es laetus, Sexte. Cūr?
   SEXTUS: Ego sum laetus quod Rōmam
   īre volō.

2. NĀRRĀTOR: Servī sunt dēfessī.
   MĀRCUS: Vōs estis dēfessī, servī. Cūr?
   SERVĪ: Dēfessī sumus quod strēnuē labōrāmus.

3. NĀRRĀTOR: Cornēlius epistulās legit.
   AURĒLIA: Quid legis, Cornēlī?
   CORNĒLIUS: Epistulās legō.

4. NĀRRĀTOR: Mārcus rāmum arripit.
   SEXTUS: Quid arripis, Mārce?
   MĀRCUS: Rāmum arripiō.

5. NĀRRĀTOR: Cornēlia rīdet.
   FLĀVIA: Cūr rīdēs, Cornēlia?
   CORNĒLIA: Rīdeō quod laeta sum.

6. NĀRRĀTOR: Senātōrēs ad urbem redeunt.
   AURĒLIA: Cūr ad urbem redītis, senātōrēs?
   SENĀTŌRĒS: Redīmus quod prīnceps nōs
   cōnsulere vult.

7. NĀRRĀTOR: Puerī lupum nōn timent.
   PUELLAE: Cūr lupum nōn timētis, puerī?
   PUERĪ: Lupum nōn timēmus quod
   temerāriī sumus.

8. NĀRRĀTOR: Puellae clāmant, "Ferte auxilium!"
   PUERĪ: Cūr vōs clāmātis "Ferte auxilium!"?
   PUELLAE: Nōs clāmāmus "Ferte auxilium!"
   quod lupum cōnspicimus.

A woman's well-groomed appearance
reflected her rank and refinement. This
Roman matron is attended by slaves
dressing her hair and holding a mirror.
Relief sculpture, Germany, circa third century A.D.

Nouns and Adjectives: Vocative

You have seen that the forms **Sexte** and **Mārce** are used when Sextus and Marcus are addressed by name. These forms are in the *vocative case*. The vocative case is used when addressing persons or things directly.

The spelling of a noun or adjective in the vocative case is usually the same as the spelling of the word in the nominative. Thus, **Cornēlia, puer**, and **pater** could be either vocative or nominative.

One exception to this rule is that 2nd declension masculine nouns such as **Sextus, Mārcus**, or **servus** and corresponding adjectives such as **magnus** or **strēnuus** change their ending to -*e* when they are used in the vocative singular, e.g., **servus** (nom.) and **serve** (voc.). Thus, among the following vocative forms only **serve** is different from the nominative:

Vocative

	1st Declension	2nd Declension			3rd Declension
Sing.	Cornēlia	serve	puer	ager	pater
Pl.	puellae	servī	puerī	agrī	patrēs

There are three other exceptions. Second declension proper names ending in **-ius**, the noun **fīlius**, *son*, and the adjective **meus**, *my*, have vocatives in -*ī*:

> *Nominative:* Cornēlius   *Vocative:* Cornēl**ī**
> *Nominative:* meus fīlius   *Vocative:* m**ī** fīl**ī**

Identify all words in the vocative in Exercise 8b.

EXERCISE 8c

Read aloud. Identify the person (1st, 2nd, or 3rd) and number (singular or plural) of each verb that is not an infinitive. Then translate:

1. Cūr ē vīllā in silvam saepe ambulātis, puellae?
2. In eādem silvā puerī quoque ambulant.
3. Īrāta sum quod servōs sedentēs cōnspiciō.
4. Arborēs ascendimus quod lupī nōs terrent.
5. "Sexte! Mārce!" clāmat Cornēlia. "Cūr nōn surgitis?"
6. "Ēheu!" inquit Dāvus. "Semper ego labōrō; semper mē vexant puerī; ad Britanniam redīre volō."
7. Omnia parāmus quod Rōmam hodiē redīmus.
8. Servī in vīllā sedent; neque Aurēliam audiunt neque respondent, nam dēfessī sunt.

   nam, conj., *for*

EXERCISE 8d

Using story 8 and the charts of forms on pages 54 and 56 as guides, give the
Latin for:

1. Slaves: "We are no longer sitting but are working hard."
2. Aurelia: "Marcus, you are still sleeping. Why are you not getting up? Why are you not preparing to return to the city?"
3. Marcus: "Why, Mother, are you waking me up? It is not yet light. I do not want to get up."
4. Aurelia: "We are preparing to return to the city today. Come on, Marcus! It is time to get up."
5. Cornelius: "Troublesome boys, why are you still sleeping? Why aren't you getting up? Why aren't you putting on your tunics and togas?"

Word Study II

Latin Bases into English Verbs

Often the bases of Latin verbs come into English with only minor changes. You can find the base by dropping the letters *-āre, -ēre, -ere,* or *-īre* from the infinitive. Replacing these letters with a silent *-e* will sometimes give you an English verb. For example, **excitāre**, base **excit-**, + silent *-e* becomes *excite* in English. Some Latin bases come into English with no change. For example, **dēscendere** (*to go down*), base **dēscend-**, produces the English *descend*.

Sometimes additional minor spelling changes occur. For example, **exclāmāre** (*to shout out*), becomes *exclaim* in English, adding an *i* in the process.

EXERCISE 1

Give an English verb derived from the base of each of these Latin verbs.
Give the meaning of each English verb. In many cases it has the same
meaning as the Latin verb:

extendere	salūtāre	revocāre	respondēre	surgere
repellere	vexāre	trādere	errāre	ascendere

Latin Bases into English Nouns and Adjectives

A Latin base may be the source of an English noun or adjective. For example, the base of **errāre** produced the Latin noun **error** and the Latin adjective **errāticus**, from which came the English *error* and *erratic*.

EXERCISE 2

The English words in italics below are derived from the bases of the Latin verbs in parentheses. Determine the meaning of the English word from the meaning of the Latin verb. Is the English word a noun or an adjective?

1. Cornelius was not moved by the runaway slave's *petition*. (**petere**)
2. Sextus's rude behavior was *repellent* to Cornelia and Flavia. (**repellere**)
3. With the *advent* of summer, Cornelius moves his family to their country house at Baiae. (**advenīre**)
4. Cornelius was dictating a letter to his *scribe*. (**scrībere**)
5. "Sextus," scolded Eucleides, "your writing is not *legible*." (**legere**)
6. The *insurgent* senators were severely punished by the emperor. (**surgere**)
7. The Roman army found the *descent* from the mountain more difficult than the *ascent*. (**dēscendere, ascendere**)

One Latin Base into Many English Words

The bases of some Latin words are the source of several English words, representing different parts of speech. For example, **urbs,** *city*, base **urb-**, is the source of:

1. *urban*   adjective, meaning "pertaining to a city"
2. *urbane*   adjective, meaning "elegant and polished in manner" (How does this idea relate to **urbs**?)
3. *urbanity*   noun, meaning "politeness, courtesy, the quality of being urbane"
4. *urbanize*   verb, meaning "to change from country to city"
5. *suburb*   noun, meaning "a residential area at the edge of a city"

EXERCISE 3

The words in each group below are derived from one Latin base. Think of a Latin word that shows this base. With its meaning in mind, determine the meaning of each English word. Finally, give the part of speech of each English word:

1. *magnate, magnificent, magnify*
2. *contemporary, tempo, temporal*
3. *prince, principal, principally*
4. *inscribe, scribble, subscribe*
5. *paternal, paternity, patron*

Go Online
PHSchool.com
Web Code: jfd-0008

PATRIA POTESTAS

Marcus's behavior shows that he respects his father's wishes and fears his displeasure just as strongly. The relationship between Roman parents and children was quite different from that in some modern societies. American children gradually become quite independent of parents by their late teens, even to the extent of choosing their marriage partner themselves. Such independence has developed only quite recently in the history of the family.

The Roman father was the supreme head (**paterfamiliās**) of his family (**familia**), which included his wife, his married and unmarried children, and his slaves. As master (**dominus**), he had the power to sell or kill his slaves. If he married his wife with full legal power (**manus**), he became owner of her property, and she ceased to belong to her own family, becoming legally a member of his. Over his children he exercised a fatherly power (**patria potestās**) that allowed him to determine their lives as he wished.

According to Roman tradition, the concept of **patria potestās** was established by the first king of Rome:

> Romulus gave the Roman father absolute power over his son. This power the father had until he died whether he imprisoned his son, whipped him, threw him into chains and made him labor on the farm, or even killed him. Romulus even let the Roman father sell his son into slavery.
>
> Dionysius of Halicarnassus, *Roman Antiquities* 2.26–27 (extracts)

The Roman father continued to have complete control even over his adult children, arranging their marriages—and divorces—and managing any property they might own. He exercised his **patria potestās** over *their* children as well.

In most instances, a father's **patria potestās** ended only with his death. A father might, however, "emancipate" his adult son, who then had **patria potestās** over his sons. A daughter who married might remain under her father's **potestās**, but her father could transfer this power into the hands of his son-in-law; such a marriage was called "marriage with **manus**" (literally, "hand").

How strictly and severely a father exercised his **potestās** varied according to personal inclination and situation. Cicero reluctantly accepted one young man as son-in-law due to the urging of his wife and of his daughter, Tullia, and he later ruefully arranged for Tullia's divorce upon her request. Another father slew his adult son in 62 B.C. because he had participated in the Catilinarian conspiracy against the Roman state. There were controls over the exercise of **patria potestās**. The slaying of a child had first to be discussed in a council of adult male relatives. Public opinion also might influence a father. Gradually, too, Roman law imposed some limits, requiring, for instance, that a daughter consent to her marriage.

True love and affection between parent and child were not eliminated by **patria potestās**. However, a father—and mother—were expected primarily to provide a moral education for their children, to prepare sons for service to the state and family through careers as magistrates, and to prepare daughters to educate and rear worthy future members of the family and state. The poet Statius, writing in the last decade of the first century A.D., congratulates his friend, Julius Menecrates, on the upbringing of his sons and daughter:

> From their father may your children learn peaceful ways and from their grandfather may they learn generosity, and from them both eagerness for glorious virtue. Because of their position and birth, the daughter will enter a noble house upon marriage, and the sons as soon as they become men will enter the threshold of Romulus's Senate house.

Statius, to Julius Menecrates (Silvae 4.8.57–62, extracts)

The tragic legend of a Roman father who felt compelled to order the execution of his own sons for disloyalty to the state is memorialized in the painting,
Lictors Bearing the Bodies of His Sons to Brutus.
Lictors Bearing the Bodies of His Sons to Brutus, *1789, Jacques-Louis David*

The consequences of disregarding a father's instructions were immortalized among the ancients in the legend of Icarus, son of Daedalus the inventor. He perished because he disobediently flew too near the sun on wings of wax his father created. Here is Dürer's engraving of that legend.
Woodcut, The Fall of Icarus, *1495*

Though the Romans may not have displayed the bond between parent and child as openly and as physically as we do, they considered it sacred: Cicero called parental love **amor ille penitus īnsitus**, "that love implanted deeply within."

A newborn child would be placed at its father's feet, and the father would accept it into the family by lifting it in his arms. Statius expressed his love for his adopted son as follows:

> He was mine, mine. I saw him lying upon the ground, a newborn baby, and I welcomed him with a natal poem as he was washed and anointed. When he demanded air for his new life with trembling cries, I set him in Life's roll.
>
> From your very moment of birth I bound you to me and made you mine. I taught you sounds and words, I comforted you and soothed your hidden hurts. When you crawled on the ground, I lifted you up and kissed you, and rocked you to sleep myself and summoned sweet dreams for you.
>
> Statius, *Silvae* 5.5.69–85 (extracts)

---

1. Family structure has differed from age to age and society to society. How would you characterize the Roman family in a few sentences?
2. What do the stories of Brutus and his sons and of Daedalus and his son Icarus have in common? How do these stories relate to the concept of **patria potestās**?
3. Parents in many societies use traditional stories to instill personal, familial, and societal values in their children. What traditional stories did your parents tell you to instill such values?

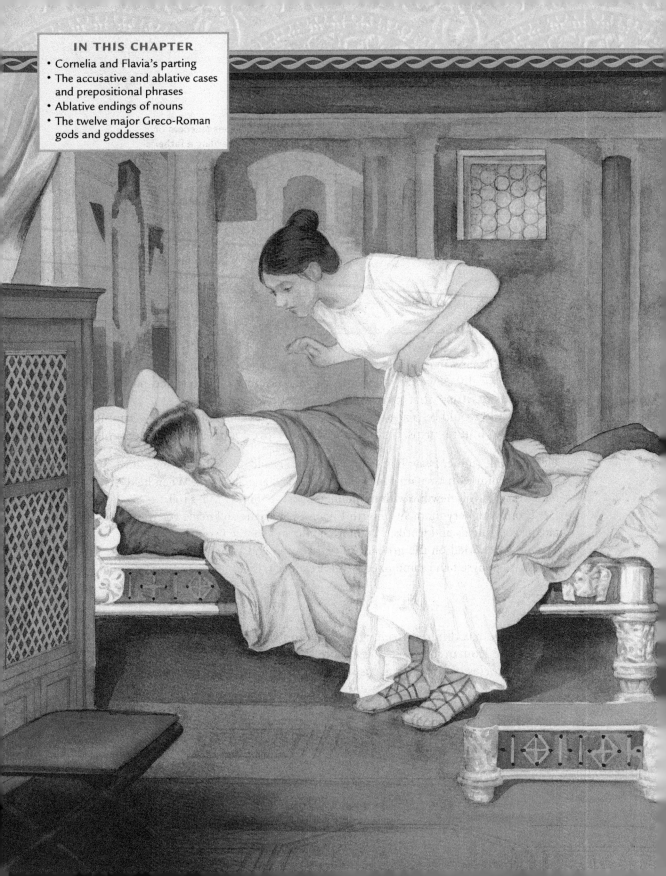

GOODBYE

Cornēlia, ubi surgit, ē vīllā suā fūrtim ambulat et per agrōs ad vīllam amīcae currit. Nōndum lūcet, sed nihil Cornēliam terret. Nēmō eam cōnspicit. Nūllī servī in agrīs labōrant. Etiam iānitor ad iānuam vīllae dormit. Cornēlia, quod tacitē intrat, iānitōrem nōn excitat.

Cornēlia cubiculum Flāviae tacitē intrat et eam excitāre temptat. Adhūc dormit   5
Flāvia. Iterum temptat Cornēlia. Flāvia sēmisomna, "Quis es? Cūr mē vexās?"

Cornēlia respondet, "Sum Cornēlia! Surge!"

Flāvia surgit. Laeta Cornēliam excipit et clāmat, "Quid tū hīc?"

Cornēlia, "Tacē, Flāvia! Nōlī servōs excitāre! Venī tacitē mēcum in agrōs. Ibi nēmō
nōs audīre potest."   10

Cornēlia Flāviam fūrtim ē vīllā in agrōs dūcit. Ubi puellae ad arborēs adveniunt,
Cornēlia, "Misera sum," inquit, "quod ego et Mārcus et Sextus et pater et māter Rōmam
hodiē redīre parāmus. Prīnceps patrem meum cōnsulere vult. Nōbīs igitur necesse est
statim discēdere."

Flāvia clāmat, "Cūr statim, Cornēlia? Cūr nōn pater tuus discēdit sōlus? Cūr   15
vōs omnēs simul discēditis?"

Respondet Cornēlia, "Nesciō, Flāvia. Sed nōbīs secundā hōrā discēdere necesse est."

Flāvia lacrimat, "Ō mē miseram! Vōs omnēs Rōmam redītis. Mihi necesse est hīc
manēre. Valē, Cornēlia! Multās epistulās ad mē mitte! Prōmittisne?"

Cornēlia, "Ego prōmittō. Et iam valē!" Cornēlia Flāviam complexū tenet et lacrimāns abit.   20

1 suā, *her own*
2 **nēmō**, *no one*
  nūllī, *no*
3 iānitor, *doorkeeper*
  ad iānuam, *at the door*
  tacitē, adv., *silently*
5 **temptat**, *(he/she) tries*
6 sēmisomna, *half-asleep*
8 **hīc**, adv., *here*
9 **Tacē!** *Be quiet!*
  Nōlī...excitāre! *Don't wake...up!*

  mēcum, *with me*
12 **misera**, *unhappy, miserable*
13 **nōbīs**, *for us*
14 **discēdere**, *to go away*
15 **tuus**, *your* (sing.)
16 vōs omnēs, *all of you*
  simul, adv., *together*
17 **nesciō**, *I do not know*
  secundā hōrā, *at the second hour*
18 **lacrimat**, *(he/she) weeps*

  Ō mē miseram! *Poor me!*
19 **manēre**, *to remain, stay*
  Valē! *Goodbye!*
  mitte, *send*
  prōmittis, *you promise*
20 complexū, *in an embrace*
  tenet, *(he/she) holds*
  lacrimāns, *weeping*
  abit, *(he/she) goes away*

EXERCISE 9a

Respondē Latīnē:

1. Cūr nēmō Cornēliam cōnspicit?
2. Quō Cornēlia Flāviam dūcit?
3. Cūr est Cornēlia misera?
4. Cūr est Flāvia misera?

Go Online PHSchool.com
Web Code: jfd-0009

Prepositional Phrases: Accusative and Ablative Cases

The meaning of sentences can be expanded by the addition of *prepositional phrases,* which usually modify verbs. Look at the examples in the columns below:

Ad vīllam redit.	*He/She returns <u>to the country house</u>.*
Ad iānuam dormit.	*He/She sleeps <u>at the door</u>.*
Per agrōs currit.	*He/She runs <u>through the fields</u>.*
Puellae prope rīvum sedent.	*The girls sit <u>near the stream</u>.*

The words underlined above form prepositional phrases, in which the prepositions **ad, per,** and **prope** are used with words in the accusative case.

You have seen other prepositions used with words in the ablative case:

Sub arbore dormit.	*He/She sleeps <u>under the tree</u>.*
Ex arbore cadit.	*He/She falls <u>out of the tree</u>.*

Note that **ex** may be written simply as **ē** when the next word begins with a consonant: **ē rāmīs,** *out of the branches.*

Now look at the following examples:

<u>In vīll**am**</u> currit.	<u>In vīll**ā**</u> sedet.
He/She runs <u>into the house</u>.	*He/She sits <u>in the house</u>.*
Statua <u>in piscīn**am**</u> cadit.	<u>In rām**ō**</u> sedet.
The statue falls <u>into the fishpond</u>.	*He/She sits <u>on the branch</u>.*
<u>In urb**em**</u> venit.	Prīnceps <u>in urb**e**</u> est.
He/She comes <u>into the city</u>.	*The emperor is <u>in the city</u>.*

In the left-hand column, the preposition **in** is used with a word in the *accusative case,* and the meaning of the preposition is *into*.

In the right-hand column, the preposition **in** is used with a word in the *ablative case,* and the meaning of the preposition is *in* or *on*.

The preposition **in** can be used with either the accusative or the ablative case, as above, but most other prepositions are used with either one case or the other.

In future vocabulary lists, prepositions will be identified with the abbreviation *prep.* followed by *acc.* or *abl.* to indicate whether the preposition is used with the accusative or the ablative case, e.g., **ad,** prep. + acc., *to, toward, at, near;* **sub,** prep. + abl., *under, beneath.*

FORMS

Nouns: Cases and Declensions

Ablative Case

Here is a chart showing the groups of nouns and cases you have met so far:

Number Case	1st Declension	2nd Declension			3rd Declension	
Singular						
Nominative	puél*la*	sérv*us*	púer	áger	páter	vōx
Accusative	puél*lam*	sérv*um*	púer*um*	ágr*um*	pátr*em*	vōc*em*
Ablative	**puéll*ā***	**sérv*ō***	**púer*ō***	**ágr*ō***	**pátr*e***	**vōc*e***
Vocative	puél*la*	sérv*e*	púer	áger	páter	vōx
Plural						
Nominative	puéll*ae*	sérv*ī*	púer*ī*	ágr*ī*	pátr*ēs*	vōc*ēs*
Accusative	puéll*ās*	sérv*ōs*	púer*ōs*	ágr*ōs*	pátr*ēs*	vōc*ēs*
Ablative	**puéll*īs***	**sérv*īs***	**púer*īs***	**ágr*īs***	**pátr*ibus***	**vōc*ibus***
Vocative	puéll*ae*	sérv*ī*	púer*ī*	ágr*ī*	pátr*ēs*	vōc*ēs*

Be sure to learn these forms thoroughly.

Note that the only difference between the nominative and ablative singular endings of 1st declension nouns is that the ablative has a long vowel: *-ā*.

EXERCISE 9b

Read aloud, identify prepositional phrases, and translate:

1. Mārcus in vīllam currit. Nūntius in vīllā est.
2. Dāvus in hortō labōrat. Mārcus in hortum festīnat.
3. Nūntius in Italiam redīre vult. Cornēlius in Italiā habitat.
4. Puer in arbore sedet. Puella in vīllam intrat.
5. In agrīs puerī ambulāre parant. Puellae in agrōs lentē ambulant.
6. In Italiā sunt multī servī. Aliī in agrīs labōrant, aliī in urbibus.
7. Servī sub arboribus sedēre volunt.
8. Servus ex arbore cadit; ad vīllam currit; in vīllā dormit.
9. Aliī nūntiī ex urbe celeriter veniunt; aliī ad urbem redeunt.
10. Puellae sub rāmīs sedent. Lupus ad puellās currit.
11. Puer ex arbore dēscendere non potest.
12. Cornēlia per iānuam in vīllam fūrtim intrat.

> **festīnat,** *(he/she) hurries*
> **aliī...aliī...,** *some...others...*

Select the correct word to fill each of the gaps, state what case each of these words is, and tell why it is in that case. Then read the sentence aloud and translate it:

1. Mārcus ad _____ sedet.   arborem/arbore
2. Puellae ē _____   silvam/silvā
   ad _____ ambulant.   vīllam/vīllā
3. Multī servī in _____ labōrant.   agrōs/agrīs
4. Cornēlia amīcam ē _____   vīllam/vīllā
   in _____ dūcit.   agrōs/agrīs
5. Servus sub _____ dormit.   rāmōs/rāmīs
6. Puerī per _____ currunt.   agrōs/agrīs
7. Cornēlius ad _____ redīre parat.   urbem/urbe
8. Flāvia prope _____ sedet.   arbore/arborem
9. Sextus ex _____ celeriter exit.   hortō/hortum
10. Servus per _____ festīnat.   agrīs/agrōs

EXERCISE 9d

In story 9, find the Latin for:

1. out of her own country house
2. through the fields
3. to (her) friend's country house
4. in the fields
5. at the door of the country house
6. into the fields
7. out of the country house
8. at the trees
9. to me

Young woman with writing tablet (tabula) and pen (stilus). Such tablets, coated with wax, were used by the Romans for writing letters such as Cornelia promises to send to Flavia.
Fresco, Pompeii, mid first century A.D.

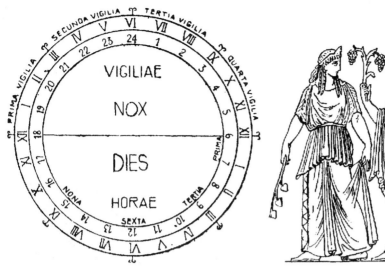

Hōrae

The Romans divided the day into twelve hours, from sunrise to sunset, and the night into four watches (*vigiliae*). Goddesses, called the *Hōrae*, regulated the orderly passage of time, the seasons, and changes of weather.

EXERCISE 9e

Review

Select, read aloud, and translate:

1. Flāvia clāmat, "Ubi _____, Cornēlia?"   estis/es
2. Cornēlia iānitōrem nōn _____.   excitāre/excitat/excitās
3. Nōs omnēs hodiē Rōmam _____.   redīre/redīmus/redītis
4. Cūr patrem _____, Mārce?   vexātis/timēs/amātis
5. Necesse est epistulās statim _____.   trādit/legere/legimus
6. Prīnceps senātōrēs _____.   cōnsulere vult/cōnsulere volunt
7. Cūr vōs omnēs simul _____?   discēdere/discēdimus/discēdere parātis
8. Tacē, Flāvia! Nōlī servōs _____.   excitāmus/excitāre/surgere
9. Cornēlia amīcam in agrōs _____.   adveniunt/dūcit/amat
10. Cūr per agrōs _____, puellae?   curritis/excitātis/curris
11. Iānitor Cornēliam nōn _____.   audiō/audiunt/audit
12. Ego nōn _____ quod
    Rōmam redīre _____.   dormīmus/surgere/surgō
    nōlō/faciunt/vidētis
13. _____ Cornēlia in agrīs nōn conspicit.   Servōs/Servī/Servus
14. Nōlī _____ excitāre!   puellās/puellae/puella
15. Senātōrēs _____ omnēs in urbe sunt.   Rōmānōs/Rōmānī/Rōmānum

Go Online
PHSchool.com
Web Code: jfd-0009

MAJOR GODS AND GODDESSES

The story of Aeneas as told on pages 28–31 is more than the story of a mortal; it involves also a number of gods and goddesses, who are shown helping or hindering Aeneas as he makes his way from Troy to Italy. Sometimes these deities are personifications of the forces of nature, such as Aeolus, who is king of the winds, and Neptune, who is lord of the sea. Jupiter, the king of the gods, intervenes at a critical moment in Aeneas's life by sending the messenger-god Mercury to deliver orders to Aeneas to leave Dido, resume his voyage, and fulfill his destiny by going to Italy. The Greeks and the Romans conceived of their gods as anthropomorphic, having the appearance, the thoughts, and the emotions of men and women, but as being greater and more powerful and above all as being immortal.

The following list gives the names of the twelve major gods and goddesses, who were thought to dwell on Mount Olympus in Greece, with their Greek names in parentheses (Latin spellings of the names are given under the illustrations on the facing page).

Jupiter (*left*) and Juno (*right*, identified by her crown and bird, the peacock) were major state gods of Rome. Both gods were worshiped in Rome and many provincial cities.
Terra cotta sculptures, Tunis, first century A.D.

| Iuppiter | Iūnō | Apollō | Mārs | Vesta | Minerva |
| Mercurius | Diāna | Neptūnus | Venus | Cerēs | Volcānus |

JUPITER (ZEUS): king of gods and mortals, wisest of the divinities, and wielder of the thunderbolt.

JUNO (HERA): queen of gods and mortals, sister and wife of Jupiter, and protectress of women and marriage.

APOLLO (PHOEBUS APOLLO): god of archery, music, medicine, and oracles. His priestesses predicted the future at Delphi (in Greece) and Cumae (in Italy).

MARS (ARES): god of war, father of Romulus and Remus.

VESTA (HESTIA): goddess of the hearth, the center of family life, and goddess of the state (a community of families), symbolized by an eternal flame guarded by six maidens ("Vestal Virgins").

MINERVA (ATHENA): goddess of wisdom, strategy in war, spinning, and weaving, creator of the olive tree, and protectress of Athens.

MERCURY (HERMES): god of travelers and thieves and messenger of the gods; he carries the caduceus, a wand twined with two snakes. On his ankles and helmet are wings. He conducts the souls of the dead to the underworld.

DIANA (ARTEMIS): twin sister of Apollo and goddess of the moon and of hunting. She is attended by a chorus of nymphs. The arc of the moon is her bow and its rays are her arrows.

NEPTUNE (POSEIDON): god of the waters and creator of the horse; his symbol is the trident, a three-pronged spear.

VENUS (APHRODITE): goddess of beauty and love, usually attended by her winged son Cupid, whose arrows strike both mortals and immortals. She was the divine mother of Aeneas, the Trojan hero and ancestor of the Romans.

CERES (DEMETER): goddess of the harvest and agriculture, whose daughter Proserpina (Persephone) is queen of the underworld and wife of Pluto (god of the underworld).

VULCAN (HEPHAESTUS): god of fire, blacksmith of the gods, and forger of the thunderbolts of Jupiter and weapons of Aeneas.

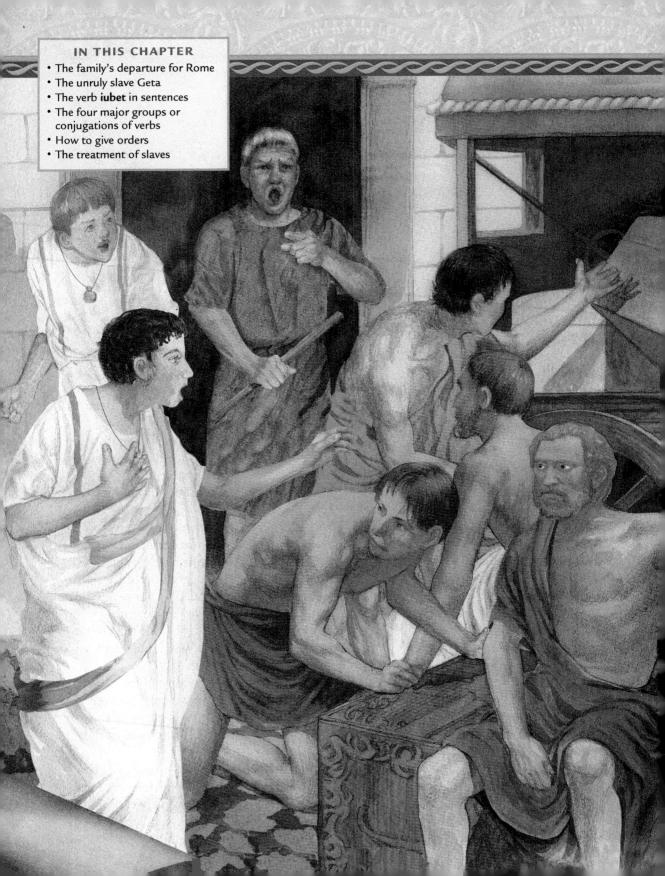

DEPARTURE

Intereā in vīllā Cornēliānā omnēs strēnuē labōrant. Aurēlia tunicam et stolam et pallam gerit. Ancillam iubet aliās tunicās et stolās et pallās in cistam pōnere. Mārcus et Sextus tunicās et togās praetextās gerunt quod in itinere et in urbe togās praetextās līberī gerere solent. Servus aliās tunicās et togās praetextās in cistam pōnit. In cubiculō Gāiī servus togās praetextās in cistam pōnit quod Gāius in urbe togam praetextam gerere 5 solet. Gāius ipse togam praetextam induit.

Dāvus, quī ipse omnia cūrat, ad iānuam stat. Servōs iubet cistās ē cubiculīs in viam portāre. Baculum habet et clāmat, "Agite, servī scelestī! Dormītisne? Hodiē, nōn crās, discēdimus."

Mārcus quoque servōs incitat et iubet eōs cistās in raedam pōnere. Servus quīdam, nōmine Geta, cistam Sextī arripit et in raedam iacit. 10

"Cavē, Geta!" exclāmat Sextus sollicitus. "Cūrā cistam meam! Nōlī eam iacere!"

Tandem omnēs cistae in raedā sunt. Ascendunt Mārcus et Sextus. Ascendit Eucleidēs. Ascendit Aurēlia. Gāius ipse ascendere est parātus. Syrus, raedārius, quoque ascendit et equōs incitāre parat. Subitō exclāmat Aurēlia, "Ubi est Cornēlia?"

Eō ipsō tempore in viam currit Cornēlia. Eam Gāius iubet in raedam statim 15 ascendere. Statim raedārius equōs incitat. Discēdunt Cornēliī.

1	**intereā**, adv., *meanwhile*	8	**baculum**, *stick*
2	**gerit**, *wears*		**habet**, *(he/she) has, holds*
	iubet, *(he/she) orders*		**scelestus**, *wicked*
	alius, *another, other*		**crās**, adv., *tomorrow*
	cista, *trunk, chest*	9	**incitat**, *(he/she) spurs on, urges on*
	pōnere, *to put, place*		**raeda**, *carriage*
3	**in itinere**, *on a journey*		servus quīdam, *a certain slave*
4	**līberī**, *children*	10	**iacit**, *(he/she) throws*
	gerere solent, *(they) are accustomed to wear(ing), usually wear*	13	**parātus**, *ready*
			raedārius, *coachman*
6	ipse, *himself*	14	**equus**, *horse*
7	**stat**, *(he/she) stands*		**Ubi...?** adv., *Where...?*
	via, *road*	15	eō ipsō tempore, *at that very moment*

EXERCISE 10a

Go Online
PHSchool.com
Web Code: jfd-0010

Respondē Latīnē:

1. Quid Aurēlia ancillam facere iubet?
2. Cūr Mārcus et Sextus togās praetextās gerunt?
3. Quid Gāius induit?
4. Quid facit Dāvus?
5. Quid clāmat Sextus?
6. Quid raedārius facere parat?
7. Quō currit Cornēlia?
8. Quid Gāius eam facere iubet?
9. Quid tum facit raedārius?
10. Quid faciunt Cornēliī?

BUILDING THE MEANING

Accusative and Infinitive

In the preceding reading, you have seen the verb **iubet** used when someone orders someone to do something. The verb is used with an accusative and an infinitive:

> Acc.   Infin.
> **Ancillam** iubet aliās tunicās et stolās et pallās in cistam **pōnere.** (10:2)
> *She orders **a slave-woman to put** other tunics and stolas and pallas into a chest.*

The infinitive **pōnere** has it own direct objects, **aliās tunicās et stolās et pallās.**

You have also seen this pattern with the verb **docet**:

> Aurēlia **Cornēliam** docet vīllam **cūrāre.** (6:11)
> *Aurelia teaches **Cornelia** (how) **to take care of** the country house.*

FORMS

Verbs: Conjugations

Latin verbs, with very few exceptions, fall into four major groups or *conjugations*. You can tell to what conjugation a verb belongs by looking at the spelling of the infinitive: (1) *-āre*, (2) *-ēre*, (3) *-ere*, and (4) *-īre*:

	1st Person Singular		Infinitive	
1st Conjugation	párō	*I prepare*	parā́re	*to prepare*
2nd Conjugation	hábeō	*I have*	habḗre	*to have*
3rd Conjugation	míttō	*I send*	míttere	*to send*
3rd Conjugation **-iō**	iáciō	*I throw*	iácere	*to throw*
4th Conjugation	áudiō	*I hear*	audī́re	*to hear*

As shown above, some verbs of the 3rd conjugation end in **-iō** in the 1st person singular, just as do verbs of the 4th conjugation. These are called 3rd conjugation **-iō** verbs. Their infinitives show that they belong to the 3rd conjugation.

Hereafter, verbs will be given in the word lists in the 1st person singular form, followed by the infinitive, e.g., **habeō, habēre,** *to have.* The infinitive will tell you to what conjugation the verb belongs. The few exceptions that do not fit neatly into any of the four conjugations will be marked with the notation *irreg.*, e.g., **sum, esse,** irreg., *to be.*

Verbs: The Present Tense

		1st Conjugation	2nd Conjugation	3rd Conjugation		4th Conjugation
Infinitive		parā́re	habḗre	míttere	iácere (-iō)	audī́re
Singular	1	párō	hábeō	míttō	iáciō	aúdiō
	2	párās	hábēs	míttis	iácis	aúdīs
	3	párat	hábet	míttit	iácit	aúdit
Plural	1	parā́mus	habḗmus	míttimus	iácimus	audī́mus
	2	parā́tis	habḗtis	míttitis	iácitis	audī́tis
	3	párant	hábent	míttunt	iáciunt	aúdiunt

Be sure to learn these forms thoroughly. Note that the vowel that precedes the personal endings is short before final -*t* and -*nt*.

In addition to **iaciō, iacere,** you have met the following **-iō** verbs of the 3rd conjugation:

arripiō, arripere   **excipiō, excipere**
cōnspiciō, cōnspicere   **faciō, facere**

Here are some examples of sentences with verbs in the present tense. Note the English translations:

a. in a simple statement of fact:
   Cornēliī Rōmam redīre **parant**.
   *The Cornelii **prepare** to return to Rome.*

b. in a description of an ongoing action:
   Hodiē Cornēliī Rōmam redīre **parant**.
   *Today the Cornelii **are preparing** to return to Rome.*

c. in a question:
   Auditne Dāvus clāmōrem?
   *Does Davus **hear** the shouting?*

d. in an emphatic statement:
   Audit clāmōrem.
   *He **does hear** the shouting.*

e. in a denial:
   Nōn **audit** clāmōrem.
   *He **does** not **hear** the shouting.*

EXERCISE 10b

Read the following verbs aloud. Give the conjugation number and meaning of each:

1. ascendō, ascendere
2. terreō, terrēre
3. arripiō, arripere
4. discēdō, discēdere
5. audiō, audīre
6. repellō, repellere
7. ambulō, ambulāre
8. excitō, excitāre
9. iaciō, iacere
10. currō, currere
11. cūrō, cūrāre
12. excipiō, excipere
13. timeō, timēre
14. nesciō, nescīre
15. rīdeō, rīdēre

EXERCISE 10c

For each of the verbs in Exercise 10b, give the six forms (1st, 2nd, and 3rd persons, singular and plural). Use the chart above as a guide. Translate the 3rd person plural of each.

Verbs: Imperative

The imperative is used in issuing orders:

Positive	Negative
Cūrā cistam meam, Geta!	**Nōlī** eam iacere, Geta!
Take care of my trunk, Geta!	*Don't throw it, Geta!* (literally, *refuse, be unwilling to throw it, Geta!*)
Cūrāte cistam meam, servī!	**Nōlīte** eam iacere, servī!
Take care of my trunk, slaves!	*Don't throw it, slaves!* (literally, *refuse, be unwilling to throw it, slaves!*)

	1st Conjugation	2nd Conjugation	3rd Conjugation		4th Conjugation
Infinitive	par*áre*	hab*ére*	mítt*ere*	iác*ere* (-iō)	aud*íre*
Imperative **Singular** **Plural**	pár*ā* par*áte*	háb*ē* hab*éte*	mítt*e* mítt*ite*	iác*e* iác*ite*	aúd*ī* aud*íte*

Be sure to learn these forms thoroughly.

Note the following imperatives, of which some forms are irregular:

dīcō, dīcere, *to say*   dīc! dīcite!
dūcō, dūcere, *to lead, take, bring*   dūc! dūcite!
faciō, facere, *to make, do*   fac! facite!
ferō, ferre, *to bring, carry*   fer! ferte!

EXERCISE 10d

For each of the following verbs, give the imperative forms, singular and plural, positive and negative. Translate each form you give:

1. pōnō, pōnere
2. ferō, ferre
3. sedeō, sedēre
4. dīcō, dīcere
5. arripiō, arripere
6. stō, stāre
7. faciō, facere
8. veniō, venīre
9. dūcō, dūcere

Go Online
PHSchool.com
Web Code: jfd-0010

TREATMENT OF SLAVES

Even though in Davus's homeland in Britain his own family had owned a few slaves, it had been difficult for him to adjust to being a slave himself. Adjust he did, however, perhaps by taking advice similar to the following given by an overseer to newly captured slaves:

> If the immortal gods wished you to endure this calamity, you must endure it with calm spirits; if you do so, you will endure the toil more easily. At home, you were free, so I believe; now as slavery has befallen you, it is best to accustom yourselves and to make it easy for your master's commands and for your own minds. Whatever indignities your master commands must be considered proper.

Plautus, The Captives 195–200

Davus enjoys a high position among Cornelius's slaves and takes pride in his responsibilities. Of course he has the good fortune to work for a master who is quite humane by Roman standards. Other slaves had more insensitive masters, who saw their slaves not as human beings but as property. Cato in his treatise on agriculture gave advice to Roman farmers on how to make a profit from their slaves. Notice that he feels no sympathy for his slaves who have grown ill or old in his service; they are "things" just like cattle and tools that a farmer should get rid of when they are no longer of use:

> Let the farmer sell olive oil, if he has a good price, also his wine and his grain.
> Let him sell his surplus too: old oxen, old tools, an old slave, a sick slave.

Cato, On Agriculture II.7 (extracts)

Some masters treated their slaves well and were rewarded by loyalty and good service, but, even when conditions were good, slaves were keenly aware of their inferior position and by way of protest sometimes rebelled or tried to run away. If they were recaptured, the letters FUG (for **fugitīvus**, *runaway*) were branded on their foreheads.

Prison cell with Roman agricultural slaves
Nineteenth-century European engraving, artist unknown

Some owners treated their slaves very badly. Even if the owner were not as bad as the despised Vedius Pollio, who fed his slaves to lampreys, slaves were liable to be severely punished, often at the whim of their master:

> Does Rutilus believe that the body and soul of slaves are made the same as their masters? Not likely! Nothing pleases him more than a noisy flogging. His idea of music is the crack of the whip. To his trembling slaves he's a monster, happiest when some poor wretch is being branded with red-hot irons for stealing a pair of towels. He loves chains, dungeons, branding, and chain-gang labor camps. He's a sadist.
>
> Juvenal, *Satires* XIV.16

Female slaves also were often subjected to ill-treatment by self-centered mistresses. Juvenal tells how a slave-woman was at the mercy of her mistress:

> If the mistress is in a bad mood, the wool-maid is in trouble, the dressers are stripped and beaten, the litter-bearers accused of coming late. The rods are broken over one poor wretch's back, another has bloody weals from the whip, and a third is flogged with the cat-o'-nine-tails. The slave-girl arranging her mistress's hair will have her own hair torn and the tunic ripped from her shoulders, because a curl is out of place.
>
> Juvenal, *Satires* VI.475

Fresco of slaves loading *amphorae*, vessels containing wine or olive oil, onto a wagon
Fresco, Pompeii, mid first century A.D.

On the other hand, Pliny the Younger speaks of owners who treated their slaves fairly and sympathetically. In a letter to a friend he writes:

> I have noticed how kindly you treat your slaves; so I shall openly admit my own easy treatment of my own slaves. I always keep in mind the Roman phrase, "father of the household." But even supposing I were naturally cruel and unsympathetic, my heart would be touched by the illness of my freedman Zosimus. He needs and deserves my sympathy; he is honest, obliging, and well educated. He is a very successful actor with a clear delivery. He plays the lyre well and is an accomplished reader of speeches, history, and poetry. A few years ago he began to spit blood and I sent him to Egypt. He has just come back with his health restored. However, he has developed a slight cough. I think it would be best to send him to your place at Forum Julii where the air is healthy and the milk excellent for illness of this kind.

> Pliny the Younger, Letters V.19

It was possible for a slave to buy his freedom if he could save enough from the small personal allowance he earned; some masters gave their slaves their freedom in a process called manumission (**manūmissiō**), as a reward for long service. A slave who had been set free was called a **lībertus** and would wear a felt cap called a **pilleus**. Many who were freed and became rich used to hide with "patches" the marks that had been made on their bodies and faces when they were slaves.

> I am very upset by illness among my slaves. Some of them have actually died, including even younger men. In cases like this I find comfort in two thoughts. I am always ready to give my slaves their freedom, so I don't think their deaths so untimely if they die free men. I also permit my slaves to make a "will," which I consider legally binding.

> Pliny the Younger, Letters VIII.16

Manūmissiō

ADDITIONAL READING:
The Romans Speak for Themselves: Book I: "Slaves and Masters in Ancient Rome," pages 33–39; "Seneca on Slavery and Freedom," pages 40–46.

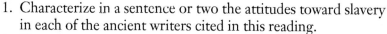

1. Characterize in a sentence or two the attitudes toward slavery in each of the ancient writers cited in this reading.
2. If you were a Roman slave owner, would you use strict discipline or relative kindness to manage your slaves? Why?

A SLAVE RUNS AWAY

Omnēs Cornēliī iam sunt in raedā. Rōmam per Viam Appiam petunt.
Intereā in vīllā Dāvus est sollicitus. Dāvus est vīlicus Cornēliī et, sī dominus abest, vīlicus ipse vīllam dominī cūrat. Dāvus igitur omnēs servōs in āream quae est prope vīllam venīre iubet. Brevī tempore ārea est plēna servōrum et ancillārum quī magnum clāmōrem faciunt. 5

Tum venit Dāvus ipse et, "Tacēte, omnēs!" magnā vōce clāmat. "Audīte mē! Quamquam dominus abest, necesse est nōbīs strēnuē labōrāre."

Tum servī mussant, "Dāvus dominus esse vult. Ecce! Baculum habet. Nōs verberāre potest. Necesse est igitur facere id quod iubet." Redeunt igitur ad agrōs servī quod baculum vīlicī timent. 10

Sed nōn redit Geta. Neque vīlicum amat neque īram vīlicī timet. Illā nocte igitur, quod in agrīs nōn iam labōrāre vult, cibum parat et ē vīllā effugit. Nēmō eum videt, nēmō eum impedit. Nunc per agrōs, nunc per viam festīnat. Ubi diēs est, in rāmīs arboris sē cēlat. Ibi dormit.

Intereā, quamquam nōndum lūcet, Dāvus omnēs servōs excitat. In agrōs exīre et ibi 15
labōrāre eōs iubet. Sed Getam nōn videt. Ubi est Geta? Dāvus igitur est īrātus, deinde sollicitus. Ad portam vīllae stat et viam spectat; sed Getam nōn videt.

1 Via Appia, *The Appian Way*	**verberō, verberāre,** *to beat*
2 **vīlicus,** *overseer, farm manager*	9 id quod, *that which, what*
dominus, *master*	11 **īra,** *anger*
3 **absum, abesse,** irreg., *to be away, be absent*	**illā nocte,** *that night*
ārea, *open space, threshing floor*	12 **effugiō, effugere,** *to flee, run away, escape*
4 **plēnus,** *full*	13 **impediō, impedīre,** *to hinder*
7 **quamquam,** conj., *although*	14 **sē cēlāre,** *to hide (himself)*
8 mussō, mussāre, *to mutter*	17 **porta,** *gate*

EXERCISE 11a

Go Online
PHSchool.com
Web Code: jfd-0011

Respondē Latīnē:

1. Quō Dāvus omnēs servōs īre iubet?
2. Quid faciunt servī et ancillae in āreā?
3. Quamquam dominus abest, quid facere necesse est?
4. Cūr necesse est facere id quod Dāvus iubet?
5. Cūr Geta effugit?
6. Ubi dormit Geta?
7. Cūr est Dāvus īrātus et sollicitus?

BUILDING THE MEANING

Go Online
PHSchool.com
Web Code: jfd-0011

The Genitive Case

You have seen how the meanings of sentences can be expanded by the addition of adjectives to modify nouns:

> Dāvus ad **magnam** portam stat.
> *Davus stands near the **large** door.*

A noun can also be modified by the addition of *another noun* in the *genitive case*.

Compare the following sentences:

Dāvus ad portam stat.	Dāvus ad portam **vīllae** stat.
Davus stands near the door.	*Davus stands near the door **of the country house**.*
Aurēlia est māter.	Aurēlia est māter **Mārcī** et **Cornēliae**.
Aurelia is a/the mother.	*Aurelia is the mother **of Marcus** and **Cornelia**.*
	*Aurelia is **Marcus** and **Cornelia's** mother.*
Servī baculum timent.	Servī baculum **vīlicī** timent.
The slaves fear the stick.	*The slaves fear **the overseer's** stick.*
In rāmīs sē cēlat.	In rāmīs **arboris** sē cēlat.
He hides in the branches.	*He hides in the branches **of the tree**.*

In the right-hand column other nouns have been added to the sentences of the left-hand column. These additional nouns are in the genitive case. This case is used to connect one noun with another to make a single phrase. The noun in the genitive case may describe another noun by indicating a family relationship, by showing possession, or by providing some other qualification or description.

Nouns in the genitive case are also used in Latin to fill out the meaning of certain adjectives. This use is parallel to the use of prepositional phrases with "of" in English:

> Ārea est <u>plēna</u> **servōrum** et **ancillārum**. (11:4)
> *The threshing floor is <u>full</u> **of slaves** and **slave-women**.*

 FORMS

Go Online
PHSchool.com
Web Code: jfd-0011

Nouns: Cases and Declensions

Genitive and Dative Cases

The following chart includes the genitive forms of 1st, 2nd, and 3rd declension nouns. It also includes the forms of the dative case. You will not study this case formally until Chapter 22. It is the case you use, for example, when you speak of giving something *to someone*. A word or phrase in the dative case can often be translated with the prepositions *to* or *for*:

> Necesse est **servīs** strēnuē labōrāre.
> *It is necessary* **for the slaves** *to work hard.*

You may wish to learn the forms of the dative case now, even though they are not formally presented until Chapter 22.

Number Case	1st Declension	2nd Declension			3rd Declension	
Singular						
Nominative	puélla	sérvus	púer	áger	páter	vōx
Genitive	**puéll**ae	**sérv**ī	**púer**ī	**ágr**ī	**pátr**is	**vṓc**is
Dative	puéllae	sérvō	púerō	ágrō	pátrī	vṓcī
Accusative	puéllam	sérvum	púerum	ágrum	pátrem	vṓcem
Ablative	puéllā	sérvō	púerō	ágrō	pátre	vṓce
Vocative	puélla	sérve	púer	áger	páter	vōx
Plural						
Nominative	puéllae	sérvī	púerī	ágrī	pátrēs	vṓcēs
Genitive	**puell**árum	servórum	puerórum	agrórum	**pátr**um	**vṓc**um
Dative	puéllīs	sérvīs	púerīs	ágrīs	pátribus	vṓcibus
Accusative	puéllās	sérvōs	púerōs	ágrōs	pátrēs	vṓcēs
Ablative	puéllīs	sérvīs	púerīs	ágrīs	pátribus	vṓcibus
Vocative	puéllae	sérvī	púerī	ágrī	pátrēs	vṓcēs

Be sure to learn the new genitive forms thoroughly.

In future vocabulary lists, nouns will be given as follows: **puella, -ae,** f., *girl*; **servus, -ī,** m., *slave*; **vōx, vōcis,** f., *voice*, i.e.:

> the nominative singular
> the genitive singular ending (**-ae, -ī**) for 1st and 2nd declension nouns
> the entire genitive singular form (**vōcis**) for 3rd declension nouns
> the gender (abbreviated as m. for masculine or f. for feminine)
> the meaning

The genitive singular ending indicates the declension to which a noun belongs: **-ae** = 1st declension, **-ī** = 2nd declension, and **-is** = 3rd declension.

The *base* of a noun is found by dropping the genitive singular ending; the other case endings are then added to this base. Note that in 3rd declension nouns, the base is often slightly different from the nominative (e.g., nominative **vōx**, base **vōc-**).

EXERCISE 11b

Translate the following sentences, completing them where necessary with reference to the family tree:

```
pater————————— māter        parentēs
(Cornēlius)      (Aurēlia)

   fīlius        fīlia        līberī
  (Mārcus)      (Cornēlia)
```

1. Mārcus est frāter Cornēliae.
2. Cornēlia est soror Mārcī.
3. Cornēlius est vir Aurēliae.
4. Aurēlia est uxor Cornēliī.
5. Mārcus est fīlius Cornēliī et Aurēliae.
6. Cornēlia est _____ Cornēliī et Aurēliae.
7. Cornēlius et Aurēlia sunt _____ Mārcī et Cornēliae.
8. Mārcus et Cornēlia sunt _____ Cornēliī et Aurēliae.
9. Aurēlia est _____ Mārcī et Cornēliae.
10. Cornēlius est _____ Mārcī et Cornēliae.

pater, patris, m., *father*
māter, mātris, f., *mother*
parēns, parentis, m./f., *parent*
frāter, frātris, m., *brother*
soror, sorōris, f., *sister*

fīlius, -ī, m., *son*
filia, -ae, f., *daughter*
līberī, līberōrum, m. pl., *children*
vir, virī, m., *man, husband*
uxor, uxōris, f., *wife*

EXERCISE 11c

Supply the genitive ending, read the sentence aloud, and translate:

1. Līberī in raedā senātōr_____ sunt.
2. Mārcus est frāter Cornēli_____.
3. Nūntius fīlium Cornēli_____ salūtat.
4. Servī īram vīlic_____ timent.
5. Effugit Geta et in rāmīs arbor_____ sē cēlat.
6. Magna vōx Dāv_____ eum terret.
7. Dāvus, vīlicus Cornēli_____, Getam vidēre nōn potest.
8. Sī Cornēlius abest, Dāvus vīllam domin_____ cūrat.
9. Magnus numerus serv_____ est in āreā.

numerus, -ī, m., *number*

EXERCISE 11d

Using story 11 and the information on the genitive case as guides, give the Latin for:

1. Davus is Cornelius's overseer, and Cornelius is Davus's master.
2. The threshing floor is full of many slaves and many slave-women.
3. The slaves fear Davus's stick.
4. Geta fears the anger of the overseer.
5. Geta sleeps in the branches of a tree.

BUILDING THE MEANING

Genitive Singular or Nominative Plural? How Do You Decide?

In the 1st and 2nd declensions, the endings of the genitive singular are the same as the endings of the nominative plural. To decide which case is being used, you will need to consider the sentence as a whole.

Look at these sentences:

1. **Celeriter redeunt servī.**

The plural verb **redeunt** raises the expectation of a plural subject, and the noun **servī** meets that expectation. In addition, the genitive usually forms a phrase with another noun. Since **servī** is the only noun in the sentence, it must be nominative plural.

2. **Pater puerī est senātor Rōmānus.**

The word **puerī** could be genitive singular or nominative plural. It must be genitive singular, since **pater** is clearly the subject of the singular verb **est**.

3. **In vīllā puellae sedent.**

The word **puellae** could be genitive singular or nominative plural. The context would help you decide whether the sentence means *The girls sit in the country house* or *They sit in the girl's country house.*

EXERCISE 11e

Look at each sentence. Is it possible to tell whether the nouns in boldface are genitive singular or nominative plural? If so, tell how. Then translate each sentence. Two of the sentences may be correctly translated two different ways:

1. **Puellae** sunt dēfessae.
2. In agrīs **puerī** ambulant.
3. **Puellae** et mātrēs in vīllā sedent.
4. **Puerī** epistulās scrībunt.
5. Pater **Mārcī** in vīllā sedet.
6. Pater vōcem **puellae** audit.
7. **Puerī** vōcem **Mārcī** audiunt.
8. Soror **puellae** per iānuam intrat.

Go Online
PHSchool.com
Web Code: jfd–0011

ROMAN NAMES

The father of the family in our story has three names, **Gāius Cornēlius Calvus**. **Gāius** is his **praenōmen** (first name or personal name), **Cornēlius** is his **nōmen** (the name of his clan), and **Calvus** (*Bald*) is his **cognōmen**, inherited from a distant ancestor. The **cognōmen** was originally a nickname but was often handed on to a man's sons and grandsons so that it came to distinguish a particular family within the larger clan. Roman society was male-oriented, and the name of a Roman boy included the **nōmen** of his father's clan and the **cognōmen** of his father's family. Thus, the name of the son in our story is **Mārcus Cornēlius Calvus**.

Women's names were far simpler. Though in early times a woman, too, might have a **praenōmen**, women came to use only the feminine form of their father's **nōmen**; thus the daughter of **Gāius Cornēlius Calvus** in our story is named simply **Cornēlia**. A second daughter would sometimes be named **Cornēlia secunda** (*the second*) or **Cornēlia minor** (*the younger*), a third daughter, **Cornēlia tertia** (*the third*), and so forth. Cornelia's mother **Aurēlia** would have been the daughter of a man who had **Aurēlius** as his **nōmen**. In the middle of the first century A.D., a little before the time of our story, women began using **cognōmina** that reflected some branch of the family tree.

In very formal naming of girls and women, the father's or husband's full name would be added in the genitive case. Thus, Cornelia would be **Cornēlia Gāiī Cornēliī Calvī** (**fīlia**) and Aurelia would be **Aurēlia Gāiī Cornēliī Calvī** (**uxor**).

In very formal naming of slaves, the master's name would be added in the genitive case, thus, **Dāvus Gāiī Cornēliī Calvī** (**servus**). As with formal naming of girls and women, the person in the genitive case represents the person who has authority, whether it be the authority of a master over a slave, of a father over a daughter, or of a husband over a wife.

Below is a transcription of the epitaph of the wife of Gnaeus Cornelius Scipio Hispallus, who served as one of the consuls, the chief magistrates of Rome, in 176 B.C. Note that he had a second **cognōmen**, and note that at this early time his wife had a **praenōmen**.

> **AVLLA·CORNELIA·CN·F·HISPALLI**
> **[P]aulla Cornēlia, Gn(aeī) f(īlia), Hispallī**
> *Paulla Cornelia, daughter of Gnaeus, (wife) of Hispallus*

1. Compare and contrast the Roman naming system with your own name and its cultural tradition.
2. How does Roman naming reflect the Romans' concern with tradition and family?
3. Romans would have been aware of the meanings of their names. Try to learn the meanings of your names.

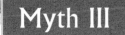

Go Online
PHSchool.com
Web Code: jfd-0011

THE FOUNDING OF ROME

The early history of Rome is a wonderful mixture of myth and fact. The Roman historian Livy admitted that his account of the founding of Rome more than 700 years before his own lifetime was based on a tradition that owed more to poetic tales than to historical fact.

The Romans traced their ancestry to the Trojan hero, Aeneas, who, as we learned in Myth I (pages 28–31), came to Italy after the fall of Troy (traditionally dated 1184 B.C.). Aeneas, after journeying through the underworld with the Sibyl of Cumae and learning of the future greatness of Rome from the ghost of his father Anchises, proceeded to Latium, the district of Italy just south of the Tiber River. There he made an alliance with Latinus, the native king, and married Lavinia, the king's daughter, to ratify the treaty. Aeneas settled the Trojans in a town he named Lavinium in honor of his new wife. Unfortunately, Turnus, king of the neighboring Rutulians and Lavinia's husband-to-be prior to Aeneas's arrival, could not accept the arrangements that Latinus made with Aeneas, and he stirred the native peoples to make war against Aeneas. Both Latinus and Turnus were killed in this war, and Aeneas then united his Trojans with the native peoples and named this Italo-Trojan nation the Latins.

Faustulus and his wife with Romulus and Remus and the she-wolf
Romulus and Remus, *oil on canvas, 1700, Charles de Lafosse*

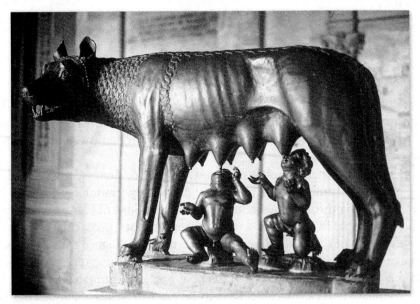

Romulus, Remus, and the she-wolf
Sculpture, Rome, fifth century B.C.

Aeneas had come from Troy with a son, Ascanius, also known as Iulus, whom Julius Caesar's family later claimed as their ancestor. After his father's death, Ascanius left Lavinium, now a strong and rich city, and established a new city that he named Alba Longa because the colony stretched out along the ridge of Mount Albanus. Ascanius's son, Silvius ("born in the woods"), succeeded his father to the throne and began the Silvian dynasty, which ruled Alba Longa for perhaps 300 years.

In the 8th century B.C. Amulius, an Alban prince, seized the throne from his older brother, Numitor; he then murdered his nephews and appointed his niece, Rhea Silvia, a priestess of Vesta (goddess of the hearth) so that she could bear no future rival heirs to the throne. When Romulus and Remus, twin sons of Rhea Silvia and the god Mars, were born, Amulius was furious. He ordered the priestess mother of the twins put into prison and gave instructions that the infants be set adrift in the Tiber. By luck, the river was in flood, and those assigned to expose Romulus and Remus happened to set the basket containing the twins in a shallow spot, expecting that it would be carried out into the mainstream and that the twins would be drowned. Attracted by the infants' crying, a she-wolf came and nursed the babies. Faustulus, the king's shepherd, discovered the wolf licking the twins and took them home to his wife. They raised Romulus and Remus as their own sons.

When Romulus and Remus grew up, they discovered their true heritage, and they then helped Numitor, their grandfather, to assassinate Amulius and regain the throne of Alba Longa.

They next decided to found a new city on the Tiber in the place where they had been exposed and raised. Since they were twins, they turned to augury and asked the gods who should give his name to this city and rule over it. On the Aventine Hill Remus saw the first omen, six vultures. No sooner had that sign been reported than a flock of twelve vultures flew over the Palatine Hill, where Romulus was standing. The followers of each twin argued whether the right to rule belonged to the one who first sighted birds or the one who sighted twice the number, and Remus died in the ensuing riot. Livy supplies an alternative version of the story: when Remus as a joke jumped over the rising city walls, Romulus was enraged and killed his brother on the spot, shouting, "This is what will happen to anyone else who jumps over my walls!" By either account, on April 21, 753 B.C. Romulus founded on the Palatine Hill that city we still call Rome.

1. Imagine you are a Roman with a traditional belief in family. What elements in the story of Romulus and Remus would trouble you and why?
2. As you continue your study of Latin, you will learn much more about mythology and religion. If this story were all you knew about the Romans' beliefs, what conclusions would you draw about Roman religion?

Archaeologists have found on the Palatine Hill the postholes for a simple hut such as this. The very first inhabitants of Rome lived in this kind of hut.

CAPTURE

Dāvus est sollicitus, nam necesse est Getam invenīre. Ubi servī effugiunt, dominī saepe vīlicōs reprehendunt. Saepe etiam eōs verberant. Cornēlius est dominus bonus, sed ubi Cornēlius īrātus est—

Servōs igitur Dāvus in āream statim convocat et rogat, "Ubi est Geta?" Nēmō respondēre potest. Dāvus igitur aliōs servōs in hortum, aliōs in agrōs, aliōs in vīneās 5 mittit. In hortō et agrīs et vīneīs Getam petunt. Neque in hortō neque in fossīs agrōrum neque in arboribus vīneārum Getam inveniunt.

Dāvus igitur servōs iubet canēs in āream dūcere. Aliī servī tunicam Getae in āream ferunt. Canēs veniunt et tunicam olfaciunt. Mox Dāvus servōs in agrōs cum canibus dūcit. Lātrant canēs. Per agrōs Cornēliī, deinde per agrōs vīcīnārum vīllārum currunt. 10 Neque rīvī neque fossae canēs impediunt. Vēstīgia Getae inveniunt, sed Getam invenīre nōn possunt. Tandem Dāvus eōs in silvam incitat.

Geta in arbore adhūc manet et ibi dormit. Canēs lātrantēs eum excitant. Nunc tamen Geta effugere nōn potest et in rāmīs sedet, immōbilis et perterritus. Canēs, ubi ad arborem appropinquant, Getam ipsum nōn cōnspiciunt, sed olfaciunt. Lātrant canēs; 15 appropinquant servī. Miserum servum vident quī in rāmīs arboris sē cēlat.

"Dēscende, Geta!" clāmat Dāvus. Geta dēscendit. Dāvus eum tunicā arripit et baculō verberat. Deinde servōs iubet Getam ad vīllam trahere et in fronte litterās FUG inūrere.

1 **inveniō, invenīre,** *to find*	**cum,** prep. + abl., *with*
2 **bonus,** *good*	10 **lātrō, lātrāre,** *to bark*
4 **convocō, convocāre,** *to call together*	11 **vēstīgia,** *tracks, footprints, traces*
rogō, rogāre, *to ask*	14 **immōbilis,** *motionless*
5 **vīnea, -ae,** f., *vineyard*	17 **tunicā,** *by the tunic*
6 **fossa,-ae,** f., *ditch*	18 **trahō, trahere,** *to drag*
8 **canis, canis,** m./f., *dog*	in fronte litterās inūrere, *to brand*
9 **ferō, ferre,** irreg., *to bring, carry*	*the letters on his forehead*
olfaciō, olfacere, *to catch the scent*	
of, smell	

EXERCISE 12a

Respondē Latīnē:

1. Cūr est Dāvus sollicitus?
2. Quō Dāvus servōs mittit?
3. Inveniuntne Getam?
4. Quid canēs faciunt?
5. Cūr Geta effugere nōn potest?
6. Ubi servī litterās FUG inūrunt?

The Ablative Case

You have learned how the meaning of sentences can be expanded by the addition of prepositional phrases, which usually modify verbs (page 64).

Prepositions used with the ablative case may modify the verbs in their sentences by answering the questions:

Ubi...?	*Where...?*
Unde...?	*From where...?*
Quōcum...? or **Quibuscum...?**	*With whom...?*

For example, questions introduced by the words at the left could be answered by statements that might include the prepositional phrases with the ablative case at the right:

Ubi...?	*Where...?*	**in vīllā**	*in the farmhouse*
Ubi...?	*Where...?*	**sub arboribus**	*under the trees*
Unde...?	*From where...?*	**ē rīvō**	*out of the stream*
Quōcum...?	*With whom...?*	**cum patre**	*with his/her father*
Quibuscum...?	*With whom...?*	**cum amīcīs**	*with his/her friends*

You will also find nouns and phrases in the ablative case without prepositions, often with predictable meanings. These also answer certain questions, as follows:

1. They may answer the question *When...?* (**Quandō...?**), in expressions referring to time:

septimā hōrā	*at the seventh hour*
nocte	*at night*
aestāte	*in the summer*
tribus diēbus	*in three days*
brevī tempore	*in a short time, soon*

This is called the *ablative of time when* or *within which*.

2. They may answer the question *How…?* (**Quō īnstrūmentō…?** or **Quōmodo…?**) and can often be translated with the words *with* or *by* and sometimes with *in*:

   a. Answering the quesion **Quō īnstrūmentō…?** *With what instrument…? By what means…? How…?*

Servum **baculō** verberat.	*with a stick*
Dāvus Getam **tunicā** arripit.	*by the tunic*
Cornēlia Flāviam **complexū** tenet.	*in an embrace*

   This is called the *ablative of instrument* or *means*.

   b. Answering the question **Quōmodo…?** *In what manner…? How…?*

Mārcus **magnā vōce** clāmat.	*with a loud voice*
	(= loudly)

   This is called the *ablative of manner* and sometimes uses a preposition, e.g., **magnā cum vōce**.

   From the very beginning of the course, you have seen another use of the ablative case:

   In pictūrā est puella, **nōmine** Cornēlia. (1:1)
   *There is a girl in the picture, Cornelia **with respect to her name/by name.***
   *There is a girl in the picture, **named** Cornelia.*

This use of the ablative without a preposition is called the *ablative of respect*.

EXERCISE 12b

Read each sentence aloud, locating the words in the ablative case and prepositional phrases with the ablative. Then translate and give in Latin the question or questions that each sentence answers:

1. Cornēlia Flāviam ē vīllā dūcit.
2. Servus molestus dominum togā arripit.
3. Secundā hōrā discēdere necesse est.
4. Dāvus magnā vōce servōs tacēre iubet: "Tacēte, omnēs!"
5. Brevī tempore ārca est plēna servōrum et ancillārum.
6. Dāvus cum servīs et canibus Getam in hortō et agrīs et vīneīs petit.
7. Vīlicus Getam baculō verberāre vult.

EXERCISE 12c

Using story 12 as a guide, answer in Latin:

1. Ubi servī Getam petunt?
2. Quibuscum servī Getam petunt?
3. Unde dēscendit Geta?
4. Quō īnstrūmentō Dāvus Getam arripit?
5. Quō īnstrūmentō Dāvus Getam verberat?

Review

Select the word or phrase in the correct case, read aloud, and translate:

1. Geta in _____ sē cēlat.   arborem/arbore/arboris
2. Prope _____ vīllae servī stant.   portae/portam/porta
3. Aliī in _____, aliī in   cubiculum/cubiculō
   _____ sedent.   āreā/āreae/āream
4. Servī in fossīs _____ Getam nōn   agrīs/agrī/agrōs
   vident.
5. Dāvus servōs in agrōs cum _____   canēs/canem/canibus
   dūcit.
6. Est magnus numerus _____ et   puerī/puerōs/puerōrum
   _____ in vīllā vīcīnā.   puellārum/puella/puellam
7. Dāvus est vīlicus _____ _____.   dominus bonus/dominō bonō/dominī bonī
8. Dāvus Getam _____ verberat.   baculum/baculī/baculō
9. Dāvus servōs iubet canēs ex _____   agrī/agrīs/agrum
   in āream dūcere.

ADDITIONAL READING:
The Romans Speak for Themselves: Book I: "The Responsibilities of a Farm Manager," pages 47–52.

"Cavē canem!"
Watchdogs were commonly chained to the wall within the entrance to a *domus*, but more often, visitors found a substitute "watchdog" depicted in the mosaic floor of the entryway.
Mosaic, second to third century A.D.

Review II: Chapters 8–12

Go Online
PHSchool.com
Web Code: jfd-0012

Exercise IIa: Nouns; Singular and Plural p. 81

Change singulars to plurals and plurals to singulars, keeping the same case:

1. vīlicō (*abl.*)
2. cistae (*gen.*)
3. noctem
4. dominī (*nom.*)
5. ancillā
6. canēs (*nom.*)
7. equōs
8. āream
9. vōx
10. fossae (*nom.*)
11. cibī (*gen.*)
12. patribus (*abl.*)
13. puerum
14. raedīs (*abl.*)
15. frontem
16. fīlius
17. portārum
18. virōrum
19. fragōrēs (*acc.*)
20. serve
21. raedāriīs (*abl.*)
22. canis (*gen.*)
23. equum
24. arbore

Exercise IIb: Verbs; Conjugations and Personal Endings   pp. 72–74

Supply the appropriate form of each of the verbs below to complete each sentence. Read the complete sentence aloud and translate it:

portō, portāre	pōnō, pōnere	inveniō, invenīre
habeō, habēre	iaciō, iacere	

Singular

1. Ego cistam _____ .
2. Tū cistam _____ .
3. Puer cistam _____ .

Plural

4. Nōs cistam _____ .
5. Vōs cistam _____ .
6. Puerī cistam _____ .

Imperatives

7. _____ cistam, puer!

8. _____ cistam, puerī!

Exercise IIc: Verbs; Identification of Forms   pp. 72–74

Give the 1st person singular, infinitive, and conjugation number of each of the following verbs. Then translate the form that is given:

For example: **surgimus**   Answer: **surgō, surgere**, 3; *we rise*

1. intrātis
2. iubēs
3. habent
4. impedīte
5. reprehendimus
6. convocā
7. rogat
8. manē
9. mussātis
10. cūrō
11. prōmittis
12. festīnāte
13. verberāmus
14. olfaciunt

Exercise IId: Prepositional Phrases with Accusative and with Ablative Cases; Ablative Case without a Preposition

pp. 64, 90–91

Complete the following sentences to match the English. Translate each sentence:

1. Cornēlia et Mārcus et Sextus _____ in vīllā habitant. (in summer)
2. Mārcus et Sextus _____ sedent. (under the tree)
3. Nūntius sollicitus _____ currit. (to the country house)
4. Puer temerārius _____ cadit. (out of the tree)
5. Cornēlia _____ ad vīllam vīcīnam fūrtim ambulat. (that night)
6. Servus _____ dormit. (at the door)
7. Cornēlius sōlus _____ epistulam scrībit. (in the country house)
8. Servī per agrōs _____ currunt. (with the dogs)
9. Statua _____ cadit. (into the fishpond)
10. Dāvus _____ Getam verberat. (with a stick)
11. Puella amīcam _____ tenet. (in an embrace)

Exercise IIe: Reading Comprehension

Read the following passage and answer the questions with complete sentences in Latin:

ON THE BANKS OF THE TIBER
IN THE EIGHTH CENTURY B.C.

In Italiā prope fluvium Tiberim habitat pastor quīdam, nōmine Faustulus. Hodiē ad casam redit et uxōrem, nōmine Accam Lārentiam, magnā vōce vocat, "Uxor! Venī celeriter ad mē!"

Lārentia venit et virum rogat, "Quid est, coniūnx? Cūr mē vocās?"

"Venī mēcum ad rīpam fluviī," respondet Faustulus. "Rem mīram tibi 5 ostendere volō. Necesse est nōbīs festīnāre."

Pastor et uxor ē casā currunt et ad Tiberim festīnant. Lārentia virum multa rogat. Vir tamen nihil respondet sed uxōrem ad rīpam fluviī dūcit. Ubi adveniunt, Lārentia rīpam spectat. Ibi videt lupam, quae puerōs geminōs alit. Lupa puerōs dīligenter cūrat et linguā lambit. 10

"Age, Faustule," clāmat Lārentia. "Rāmum arboris arripe et lupam repelle!"

"Cūr mē lupam repellere iubēs?" rogat vir. "Lupa puerōs neque vexat neque terret. Ecce! Puerōs cūrat quod eōs amat."

"Ita vērō," respondet uxor, "sed ego puerōs ad casam nostram portāre volō. Ego et tū puerōs velut līberōs nostrōs cūrāre dēbēmus." 15

Faustulus ad lupam appropinquat. Eam rāmō repellere parat. Lupa tamen neque lātrat neque pastōrem petit sed puerōs lambit et in silvam effugit. Tum pastor et uxor puerōs ad casam portant. "Sine dubiō," exclāmat Faustulus, "sunt puerī mīrābilēs."

1 fluvius, -ī, m., *river*
  Tiberis, Tiberis, m., *the Tiber River*
  pastor, pastōris, m., *shepherd*
2 casa, -ae, f., *hut, cottage*
  vocō, vocāre, *to call*
4 coniūnx, coniugis, m./f., *spouse,*
     husband or *wife*
5 rīpa, -ae, f., *bank*
  rem mīram, *a wonderful thing*
  tibi, *to you*
6 ostendō, ostendere, *to show*
7 multa, *many things*

9 geminus, *twin*
  alō, alere, *to feed, nourish*
10 dīligenter, *carefully*
   lingua, -ae, f., *tongue*
   lambō, lambere, *to lick*
14 noster, *our*
15 velut, adv., *just as*
   dēbēmus, *we ought*
17 petō, petere, *to look for, seek, attack*
18 sine dubiō, *without a doubt*
19 mīrābilis, *extraordinary, wonderful*

1. Who is Faustulus?
2. Whom does he call with a loud voice?
3. To what place is it necessary to hurry?
4. What does Larentia see when she gets there?
5. What is the she-wolf doing?
6. What does Larentia want to do with the boys?
7. What are the last two things that the she-wolf does?
8. What, in Faustulus's judgment, are the boys?

Exercise IIf: Identification of Forms

In the passage on page 94, identify the following:

1. One 1st person singular verb.
2. Two 2nd person singular verbs.
3. One 1st person plural verb.
4. Three imperatives.
5. Three words in the genitive case and the noun that each modifies.
6. Three prepositional phrases with the accusative case.
7. Three prepositional phrases with the ablative case.
8. Four uses of the ablative case without a preposition.

DISASTER

Intereā Cornēliī per Viam Appiam iter faciēbant. Cornēlius, quod ad urbem tribus diēbus advenīre volēbat, Syrum identidem iubēbat equōs incitāre. Syrus igitur equōs virgā verberābat. Dum per viam ībant, Aurēlia et Cornēlia spectābant rūsticōs quī in agrīs labōrābant. Mārcus et Sextus spectābant omnēs raedās quae per Viam Appiam ībant. 5

Septima hōra erat. Diēs erat calidus. In agrīs rūsticī nōn iam labōrābant sed sub arboribus quiēscēbant. In raedā Cornēlius et Aurēlia iam dormiēbant. Mārcus pede vexābat Cornēliam quae dormīre volēbat. Sextus cum raedāriō Syrō sedēbat; viam et vehicula spectābat.

Subitō, "Ecce, Mārce!" exclāmat Sextus. "Est aurīga!" 10

Mārcus magnō rīsū respondet, "Nōn est aurīga, fatue! Est tabellārius quī epistulās cīvium praeclārōrum ab urbe fert. Tabellāriī semper celeriter iter faciunt quod epistulās ab urbe ad omnēs partēs Italiae ferunt."

"Quam celeriter iter facit!" clāmat Sextus. "Equōs ferōciter virgā incitat. Cavē tabellārium, Syre! Tenē equōs! Cavē fossam! Cavē fossam!" 15

Syrus equōs tenet et tabellārium vītat, sed raeda in fossam magnō fragōre dēscendit.

1 **iter,** *journey*
  iter faciēbant, *(they) were traveling*
2 tribus diēbus, *in three days*
  volēbat, *(he/she) wanted*
  identidem, adv., *again and again*
  iubēbat, *(he) ordered, kept ordering*
3 virga, -ae, f., *stick, switch*
  verberābat, *(he) kept beating, whipping*
  ībant, *(they) were going*
  rūsticus, -ī, m., *peasant*
6 septimus, *seventh*
  erat, *(it) was*
7 **quiēscēbant,** *(they) were resting*
  pēs, pedis, m., *foot*

9 **vehicula,** *vehicles*
10 **aurīga, -ae,** m., *charioteer*
11 **magnō rīsū,** *with a loud laugh*
  fatuus, *stupid*
  tabellārius, -ī, m., *courier*
12 **cīvis, cīvis,** gen. pl., **cīvium,** m./f., *citizen*
  praeclārus, *distinguished*
  ab or **ā,** prep. + abl., *from*
13 **pars, partis,** gen. pl., **partium** f., *part*
14 **Quam…!** adv., *How…!*
  ferōciter, adv., *fiercely*
  Cavē…! *Watch out (for)…!*
16 **vītō, vītāre,** *to avoid*

EXERCISE 13a

Respondē Latīnē:

1. Quid Cornēliī faciēbant?
2. Cūr Cornēlius Syrum identidem iubēbat equōs incitāre?
3. Cūr rūsticī nōn iam labōrābant?

4. Quis celeriter appropinquat?
5. Vītatne Syrus tabellārium?
6. Quō dēscendit raeda?

Go Online
PHSchool.com
Web Code: jfd-0013

3rd Declension i-stem Nouns

Some 3rd declension nouns such as **cīvis** and **pars** end in *-ium* instead of *-um* in the genitive plural. These are called *i-stem nouns*, and they will be identified in vocabulary lists by inclusion of the genitive plural form.

Verbs: The Imperfect Tense I

Up to the beginning of this chapter all of the verbs in the Latin stories described actions that were going on in the present with respect to the time of the story. All of these verbs are said to be in the present tense. (The word tense came into English from Old French *tens*, "tense," "time," which came from the Latin **tempus,** *time*.) Tense refers to the time when an action is conceived as taking place.

Look at the following sentences from the story at the beginning of this chapter:

Per Viam Appiam iter **faciēbant.** (13:1)	*They **were traveling** along the Appian Way.*
Ad urbem tribus diēbus advenīre **volēbat.** (13:1–2)	*He **wanted** to reach the city in three days.*
Syrus equōs **verberābat.** (13:2–3)	*Syrus **kept whipping** the horses.*

The Latin verbs in bold type are examples of the *imperfect tense*. This tense is easily recognized by the tense sign *-ba-* that appears before the personal endings. The verbs in the imperfect tense in these sentences describe actions that took place in past time and that were continuous or repeated.

N.B. The imperfect forms of **sum, esse,** *to be*, and **possum, posse,** *to be able*, are irregular. They may be recognized by the letters **era-:**

erat, *(he/she/it) was*   **poterat,** *(he/she/it) was able*
erant, *(they) were*   **poterant,** *(they) were able*

EXERCISE 13b

Read aloud, say whether the verb is present or imperfect, and translate:

1. Cornēlia sub arbore sedet.
2. Flāvia in agrīs ambulābat.
3. Rōmānī in Italiā habitant.
4. Servī Getam invenīre nōn poterant.
5. Lātrant canēs; appropinquant servī.
6. Mārcus et Sextus raedās spectābant.
7. Erant rūsticī prope Viam Appiam.
8. Puerī saepe currunt in agrīs.
9. Geta labōrāre nōlēbat.
10. Tabellāriī epistulās ab urbe in omnēs partēs Italiae ferēbant.

EXERCISE 13c

Using story 13 and the information on the imperfect tense as guides, give the
Latin for:

1. Again and again Cornelius kept ordering Syrus to spur on the horses.
2. The day was warm, and it was the seventh hour.
3. The peasants were resting under the trees, and Cornelius and Aurelia were asleep
   in the carriage.
4. Marcus was sitting in the carriage and annoying Cornelia with his foot.
5. Sextus was looking at a courier who was going along the road.

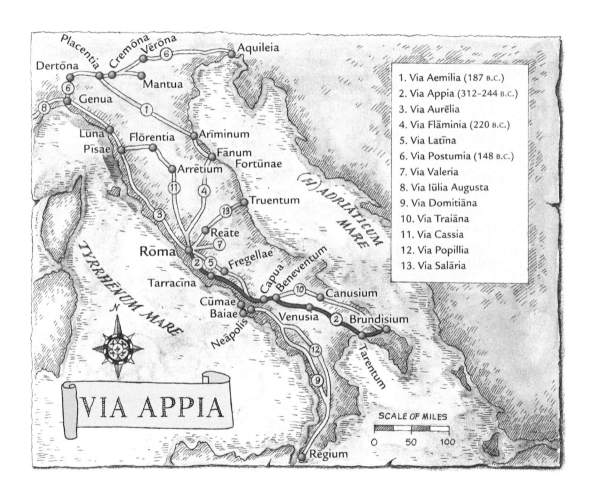

BUILDING THE MEANING

Adverbs

You have seen a number of ways in which the meaning of simple Latin sentences can be expanded by the addition of modifiers. One commonly used modifier is the *adverb*. Adverbs can modify verbs ("She ran *quickly*"), adjectives ("She is *very* beautiful"), or other adverbs ("She ran *very* quickly").

Latin adverbs are sometimes formed from adjectives by using the ending *-ē* or *-iter*:

Adjective	Adverb
strēnuus, *active, energetic*	**strēnuē,** *strenuously, hard*
celer, *quick*	**celeriter,** *quickly*

But you have met many adverbs that are not formed from adjectives and do not have these endings. See the lists below.

Adverbs often indicate the *time, place,* or *manner* of the action of the verb:

Time:
Mārcus **adhūc** dormit.
*Marcus is **still** sleeping.*

Others:
crās, *tomorrow*
deinde, *then, next*
hodiē, *today*
iam, *now, already*
identidem, *again and again, repeatedly*
intereā, *meanwhile*
iterum, *again, a second time*
mox, *soon, presently*
nōn iam, *no longer*

nōndum, *not yet*
nunc, *now*
saepe, *often*
semper, *always*
simul, *together, at the same time*
statim, *immediately*
subitō, *suddenly*
tandem, *at last, at length*
tum, *at that moment, then*

Place:
"Quid tū **hīc**?" (9:8)
*"What (are) you (doing) **here**?"*

Other:
ibi, *there*

Manner:

Sextus **celeriter** tunicam et togam induit. (8:9–10)
*Sextus **quickly** puts on his tunic and toga.*

Others:
>   **ferōciter,** *fiercely*
>   **fūrtim,** *stealthily*
>   **lentē,** *slowly*
>   **strēnuē,** *strenuously, hard*
>   **tacitē,** *silently*

Other Adverbs:
>   **etiam,** *also, even*
>   **Ita vērō!** *Yes! Indeed!*
>   **Minimē!** *No! Not at all!*
>   **nōn,** *not*
>   **Quam...!** *How...!*
>   **quoque,** *also*
>   **tamen,** *however, nevertheless*

Note that some of the adverbs on the previous page and above end with letters that are used in case endings of nouns and adjectives: **-ās, -e, -am, -em, -ā, -um,** and **-ō.** Be sure that you know that the words on these pages are adverbs and not nouns or adjectives.

Rome

Some sections of the ancient Appian Way have survived over time. The wheel ruts shown in the picture are the result of the heavy traffic over the road throughout the centuries.
Via Appia Antica, Rome

Word Study III

Latin Suffix -*or*

The suffix -*or*, when added to the base of a Latin verb, creates a 3rd declension noun that means "the act of" or "the result of" that particular verb. The base of a verb is found by dropping the -*āre*, -*ēre*, -*ere*, or -*īre* ending from its infinitive. For example, **clāmāre** (base: **clām-**) becomes **clāmor, clāmōris** m., *shouting*. The Latin noun formed in this way often comes into English unchanged. The derivative *clamor* means "a loud outcry."

EXERCISE 1

Create a 3rd declension noun from each verb below. Give the nominative and genitive singular of the noun. Give an English derivative, if there is one.

terrēre	**tenēre**	**stupēre** (*to be amazed*)
errāre	**timēre**	**valēre** (*to be strong*)

English Suffix -*(i)fy*

The Latin verb **facere**, *to make, do*, is the source of the English verb suffix -*(i)fy*, meaning "to make." The English word *beautify* means "to make beautiful." Often the base to which the suffix is added is also of Latin origin. The Latin word **magnus** provides the base for the English word *magnify*, "to make large."

EXERCISE 2

Give the English verbs made by adding the suffix -*(i)fy* to the bases of these Latin words.

terrēre	**satis** (*enough*)
quālis	**ūnus** (*one*)
nūllus	**signum** (*sign*)

EXERCISE 3

Match each English word in the column at the left with its meaning in the column at the right. Use the meaning of the Latin word in parentheses as a guide.

1. *fraternity* (**frāter**)
2. *novelty* (**novus**)
3. *pedestrian* (**pēs, pedis**)
4. *procrastinate* (**crās**)
5. *ancillary* (**ancilla**)
6. *tacit* (**tacitē**)
7. *simultaneous* (**simul**)
8. *dominate* (**dominus**)

a. unspoken
b. put off until tomorrow
c. brotherhood
d. be master over
e. traveler on foot
f. something new
g. at the same time
h. serving as helper

Latin Mottoes

Although Latin is an ancient language, its words and phrases are still part of our life today. Look at the inscriptions on a penny, nickel, dime, or quarter. Find the Latin words E PLURIBUS UNUM. This is the motto of the United States, meaning "out of many, one." It refers to the many colonies that were united to make one nation.

Many states, universities, and other organizations have Latin mottoes, which serve as symbols of their purpose, for example:

SEMPER FIDELIS *always faithful* (U.S. Marine Corps)

VOX CLAMANTIS IN DESERTO *the voice of one crying in the wilderness*
    (Dartmouth College)

VERITAS VOS LIBERABIT *the truth will set you free* (Johns Hopkins University)

NIL SINE MAGNO LABORE *nothing without great effort* (Brooklyn College)

MIHI CURA FUTURI *I care for the future* (Hunter College)

VOLENS ET POTENS *willing and able* (4th Army Engineers)

IN ARDUIS FIDELIS *faithful in adversity* (Medical Corps)

AD ASTRA PER ASPERA *to the stars through difficulties* (Kansas)

DUM SPIRO, SPERO *while I breathe, I hope* (South Carolina)

CAVEAT EMPTOR *let the buyer beware* (proverb)

CARPE DIEM *seize the day* (Horace)

COGITO ERGO SUM *I think, therefore I am* (Descartes)

ERRARE HUMANUM EST *to err is human* (Seneca)

ARS LONGA, VITA BREVIS *art is long, but life is brief* (Horace)

FESTINA LENTE *make haste slowly* (Augustus)

O TEMPORA! O MORES! *O the times, O the values!* (Cicero)

A MARI USQUE AD MARE *from sea to sea* (national motto of Canada)

GRANDESCUNT AUCTA LABORE *by work, all things increase and grow*
    (McGill University)

EXERCISE 4

Find further examples of mottoes in English, Latin, or other languages used by any of the following:

a. your home state or city
b. military units, such as the army, navy, or air force
c. local colleges, universities, or academies
d. local organizations: community service groups, political groups, unions, or clubs

Make up a motto for your family, best friend, pet, favorite movie star, or sports hero.

WHO IS TO BLAME?

Ubi dēscendit raeda in fossam, concidunt omnēs. Nēmō tamen ē raedā cadit. Mox cūnctī in viam ē raedā dēscendunt, sollicitī sed incolumēs. Cornēlius, quamquam gaudet quod omnēs sunt incolumēs, raedārium miserum reprehendit.

"Age, Syre! Nōlī cessāre! Extrahe statim raedam ē fossā!"

Syrus igitur equōs incitat. Equī raedam strēnuē trahunt, sed frūstrā. Raeda in fossā   5
haeret immōbilis. Syrus eam movēre nōn potest.

"Ō sceleste!" inquit Cornēlius. "Tuā culpā raeda est in fossā. Quid tū faciēbās ubi cisium appropinquābat? Dormiēbāsne?"

Interpellat Sextus, "Syrus nōn dormiēbat, sed per viam placidē ībat dum appropinquābat cisium. Ego et Mārcus spectābāmus cisium, quod celerrimē appropinquābat.   10
Deinde tabellārius equōs ad raedam nostram dēvertēbat. Perīculum erat magnum. Syrus cisium vītāre poterat et iam nōs omnēs sumus incolumēs quod Syrus raedam magnā arte agēbat."

Tum Cornēlius rogat, "Tūne cisium spectābās, Mārce, ubi appropinquābat?"

"Ita vērō, pater!" respondet Mārcus. "Omnia observābam. Erat culpa tabellāriī, nōn   15
Syrī. Syrus raedam magnā arte agēbat."

Sed Cornēlius, magnā īrā commōtus, virgam arripit et raedārium miserum verberat.

1 **concidō, concidere,** *to fall down*
2 **cūnctī,** *all*
  incolumis, *unhurt, safe and sound*
  gaudeō, gaudēre, *to be glad*
3 **quod,** conj., with verbs of feeling, *that*
4 **cessō, cessāre,** *to be idle, do nothing*
  extrahō, extrahere, *to drag out*
5 **frūstra,** adv., *in vain*
6 **haereō, haerēre,** *to stick*
  moveō, movēre, *to move*
7 **culpa, -ae,** f., *fault, blame*
    tuā culpā, *because of your fault, it's
      your fault that*

8 **cisium,** *light two-wheeled carriage*
9 **interpellō, interpellāre,** *to interrupt*
  placidē, adv., *gently, peacefully*
10 **quod,** *which*
  celerrimē, adv., *very fast*
11 **noster,** *our*
  dēvertēbat, *he began to turn aside*
  perīculum, *danger*
12 **ars, artis,** gen. pl., **artium,** f., *skill*
13 **agō, agere,** *to do, drive*
14 **Tūne…spectābās,** *Were you
    watching?*
17 **commōtus,** *moved*

EXERCISE 14a

Respondē Latīnē:

1. Quid accidit ubi raeda in fossam dēscendit?
2. Cūr Cornēlius gaudet?
  accidit, *happens*

3. Dormiēbatne Syrus ubi cisium appropinquābat?
4. Quōmodo commōtus est Cornēlius?

Go Online
PHSchool.com
Web Code: jfd-0014

Verbs: The Imperfect Tense II

You have now met all the endings of the imperfect tense:

Singular			Plural		
	1	-bam		1	-bāmus
	2	-bās		2	-bātis
	3	-bat		3	-bant

Note that the vowel is short before final *-m, -t,* and *-nt.*

These are the endings of the imperfect tense of *all* Latin verbs (except **esse** and its compounds, of which **posse** is one; see page 98).

Compare the following chart showing verbs in the imperfect tense with the chart showing present tense forms on page 73.

		1st Conjugation	2nd Conjugation	3rd Conjugation		4th Conjugation
Infinitive		par*ā́re*	hab*ḗre*	mítt*ere*	iác*ere* (-iō)	aud*ī́re*
Singular	1	parā́*bam*	habḗ*bam*	mittḗ*bam*	iaciḗ*bam*	audiḗ*bam*
	2	parā́*bās*	habḗ*bās*	mittḗ*bās*	iaciḗ*bās*	audiḗ*bās*
	3	parā́*bat*	habḗ*bat*	mittḗ*bat*	iaciḗ*bat*	audiḗ*bat*
Plural	1	parābā́*mus*	habēbā́*mus*	mittēbā́*mus*	iaciēbā́*mus*	audiēbā́*mus*
	2	parābā́*tis*	habēbā́*tis*	mittēbā́*tis*	iaciēbā́*tis*	audiēbā́*tis*
	3	parā́*bant*	habḗ*bant*	mittḗ*bant*	iaciḗ*bant*	audiḗ*bant*

Be sure to learn these forms thoroughly.

Note that the personal endings are the same as those given for the present tense on page 54, except that in this tense the 1st person singular ends in *-m* (compare **sum**).

The imperfect tense shows action *in the past* that was

    a. going on for a time:

        Ego et Mārcus **spectābāmus** cisium. (14:10)
        Marcus and I were watching the carriage.

        Cornēlia dormīre **volēbat**. (13:8)
        Cornelia wanted to sleep.

    b. repeated:

        Mārcus **vexābat** Cornēliam. (13:7–8)
        Marcus kept annoying Cornelia.

    c. habitual or customary:

        Dāvus in Britanniā **habitābat**.
        Davus used to live in Britain.

d. beginning to happen:

> Equōs ad raedam nostram **dēvertēbat.** (14:11)
> He **began to turn** the horses **aside** in the direction of our carriage.

Let the context guide you to an appropriate translation.

EXERCISE 14b

Read aloud, paying special attention to the tenses of verbs. Then translate:

1. Tabellārium līberī spectābant.
2. Cornēlius, ubi epistulās scrībēbat, uxōrem et līberōs vidēre nōlēbat.
3. Gaudēbat Cornēlius quod omnēs incolumēs erant.
4. Cīvēs tabellāriōs ex urbe saepe mittunt.
5. Syrus tabellārium vītāre poterat quod equōs tenēbat.
6. Dormiēbāsne, Syre? Minimē vērō, domine! Ego placidē per viam ībam.
7. Quid vōs faciēbātis, puerī? Nōs omnēs raedās spectābāmus, pater.
8. Appropinquābatne cisium placidē? Minimē! Celerrimē per viam ībat.
9. Cūr mē semper vexās, Mārce? Dormīre volō.

EXERCISE 14c

Select, read aloud, and translate:

1. Tabellārius equōs ferōciter _____.   incitābam/incitābat/incitābant
2. Pater et māter ē raedā _____.   dēscendēbās/dēscendēbat/dēscendēbant
3. Cūr tū celeriter iter _____?   faciēbās/faciēbant/faciēbāmus
4. Nōs omnēs in raedā _____.   dormiēbam/dormiēbātis/dormiēbāmus
5. Ego et Mārcus saepe in agrīs _____.   currēbāmus/currēbant/currēbat

EXERCISE 14d

Supply the appropriate imperfect tense endings, read aloud, and translate:

1. Tabellārius multās epistulās ab urbe portā_____.
2. Cornēlia, quae dēfessa era_____, in cubiculō dormiē_____.
3. Nōs raedās magnā arte agē_____.
4. Sub arboribus vīneārum et in olīvētīs vōs Getam petē_____.
5. Latrā_____ canēs; per agrōs curre_____; Getam invenīre nōn potera_____.
6. "Servumne, Dāve, baculō verberā_____?"
7. Aliī servī in vīllā, aliī in vīneīs labōrā_____.
8. Sextus identidem clāmā_____, "Ecce! Aurīga!"

olīvētum, *olive grove*

Verbs: Irregular Verbs I

The infinitives of a few Latin verbs show that they do not belong to one of the four regular conjugations. They are therefore called *irregular verbs*. Two of these are the verbs **sum, esse**, *to be*, and **possum, posse**, *to be able*; *I can*, a verb consisting of **pos-** or **pot-** + the forms of **sum**:

	Present	Imperfect	Present	Imperfect
Infinitive	ésse		pósse	
Singular 1	sum	éram	póssum	póteram
2	es	érās	pótes	póterās
3	est	érat	pótest	póterat
Plural 1	súmus	erắmus	póssumus	poterắmus
2	éstis	erắtis	potéstis	poterắtis
3	sunt	érant	póssunt	póterant

Be sure to learn these forms thoroughly.

EXERCISE 14e

From the chart above, select the verb form that will complete the Latin sentence to match the English cue. Then read aloud and translate the entire sentence:

1. Dāvus sollicitus est, nam Getam invenīre nōn _____. (*is able/can*)
2. Tū _____ raedārius scelestus, Syre! (*are*)
3. Flāvia misera erat quod Cornēlia in vīllā manēre nōn _____. (*was able/could*)
4. Vōs incolumēs _____ quod Syrus equōs magnā arte agēbat. (*are*)
5. Getam, Dāve, in agrīs invenīre nōs nōn _____. (*were able/could*)
6. Canēs, quī Getam olfacere _____, lātrant. (*are able/can*)
7. Quamquam Cornēlius _____, servī strēnuē labōrābant. (*was away*)
8. Ō mē miserum! Quō īnstrūmentō ego raedam ē fossā extrahere _____? (*am able/can*)
9. Equī cisium sed nōn fossam vītāre _____. (*were able/could*)
10. Dāvus vōs verberāre vult, nam Getam invenīre vōs nōn _____. (*were able/could*)

EXERCISE 14f

Using story 14 and the material on verbs in this chapter as guides, give the Latin for:

1. Although all were unhurt, Cornelius was scolding the coachman.
2. Cornelius: "Why were you not able to drag the coach out of the ditch, Syrus?"
3. Syrus and Sextus: "We were not sleeping when the light carriage was approaching."
4. Cornelius: "Were you watching the light carriage that was approaching very fast, Syrus and Sextus?"
5. Syrus and Sextus: "We were able to avoid the light carriage, and although we are in the ditch we are all unhurt."

THE KINGS OF ROME

According to legend, seven kings ruled Rome over a span of 243 years. Myth, legend, and history are intertwined in the accounts of their rule.

Romulus, as the founding king, devised a set of laws for his Romans, a group of fellow shepherds and a motley crew of rough men who had come together to start new lives in a new place for a variety of reasons. They could not very well found a society, however, without women and the prospect of children.

When ambassadors who had been sent to arrange marriage treaties with neighboring states returned empty-handed, rebuffed, and ridiculed, Romulus adopted a bold plan. He invited these neighbors to a grand festival in honor of Neptune. Largely out of curiosity and a desire to see the new city, many came to Rome, including Sabines who brought along their whole families. Impressed by the grand tour, the guests sat attentively, watching the spectacle. At a signal from Romulus, suddenly the young Roman men rushed in and carried off the young unmarried Sabine girls. Most grabbed the first potential bride they encountered. A few senators had their followers grab some of the especially pretty ones they had picked out ahead of time.

Romulus and the other Romans persuaded the Sabine women, with assurances of deep love and lasting marriages, to accept their new roles as Roman wives (**mātrōnae**). Their families, who had fled from the fracas, attacked Rome to reclaim their daughters. As the Sabine and Roman armies opened battle on the future site of the Roman Forum, however, the Sabine women intervened and begged them to stop fighting, saying they did not wish to become both widows and orphans on the same day. In response, the Sabines and Romans united to form one state with Rome as the capital city.

After the second king of Rome, Numa Pompilius, had devoted much attention to legal and religious institutions, the third king, Tullus Hostilius, renewed the state's emphasis on its military posture. Tullus declared war on the Albans because of cattle-raiding. Both sides agreed to settle the conflict by having the Horatii, a set of Roman triplets, battle a set of Alban triplets, the Curiatii. As their armies watched, the two sets of triplets clashed. Two of the Romans died; all three Albans were wounded. Outnumbered three to one, but unscathed, the surviving Roman, Horatius, took flight, counting on the strategic assumption that the three Curiatii would pursue him and thus be separated. One by one he was able to turn back and face each of his foes until he had dispatched all three Albans and Rome claimed victory.

When the Albans later proved disloyal and tried to desert the Romans in a battle against the cities of Fidenae and Veii, Tullus destroyed Alba Longa and moved her citizens to Rome. But as Tullus prepared further campaigns, he fell ill and turned to religion for deliverance from a plague. Legend has it that he performed a sacrifice to Jupiter incorrectly and consequently was struck by a bolt of lightning, perishing in flames with his palace.

Ancus Marcius, grandson of Numa, who was elected the fourth king of Rome, turned his attention to major construction projects: new city walls, a prison, a bridge across the Tiber (the **Pōns Sublicius** or bridge built on piles), and the seaport of Rome at Ostia, located at the mouth of the Tiber River.

The fifth king of Rome, Lucius Tarquinius Priscus, from Etruria to the north of Rome, gained the throne by fraud and was subsequently murdered at the instigation of the sons of Ancus Marcius. Priscus's wife, Tanaquil, then engineered the ascent to the throne of her daughter's husband, Servius Tullius.

Servius was a much respected king. After he solidified his status with a victory in war against Veii, he went to work on the organization of Roman society. He held the first census and established the practice of assigning all Roman citizens to classes based on wealth. He further enlarged the physical boundaries of Rome to accommodate the increased population, bringing the city to its total of seven hills.

Palace intrigues, however, continued. Tullia, Servius's daughter, engineered the murder of her sister and her own husband and then goaded her new husband, Lucius Tarquinius, into proclaiming himself King Tarquinius and confronting her father before the Roman senate. Tarquinius threw Servius out of the Senate House bodily, and his agents murdered the king in the street. Tullia arrived to be the first to hail her husband the seventh king of Rome. Heading home, she ordered her horrified carriage driver to run over the body of her father lying in the road—an act immortalized by the street's name, **Vīcus Scelerātus** (Street of Crime).

That seventh and final king of Rome soon earned his name Tarquinius Superbus, Tarquin the Proud, by executing many senators and refusing to seek the counsel of that body. He did achieve military successes and oversaw construction of the great temple of Jupiter on the Capitoline hill and the **cloāca maxima**, the main sewer of Rome. But the penchant for crime continued to run in the veins of

To settle the dispute between Rome and Alba Longa, the three Horatii brothers swear, in the presence of their father, mother, and sisters to fight the three Curiatii brothers.
The Oath of the Horatii, *oil on canvas, 1784, Jacques-Louis David*

Sextus demands that Lucretia yield to him (*left*). Lucretia's husband and friends find her overcome with shame (*right*). Lucretia's body is shown to the Romans, and Brutus demands that they avenge her (*center*).
The Tragedy of Lucretia, *oil on wood, ca. 1500–1501, Sandro Botticelli*

the Tarquin family. The youngest son, Sextus Tarquinius, developed a passion for Lucretia, the wife of his cousin, Tarquinius Collatinus, and raped her. Lucretia, after telling her husband, father, and Lucius Junius Brutus what had happened, stabbed herself and died. That was cause enough to inspire Brutus, Collatinus, and other worthy Romans to persuade the citizens to oust Tarquinius Superbus and everyone in his family and to replace the kingship with a new form of government, the Republic. This was accomplished in 509 B.C.

Fact and fiction are intertwined in these legends from the age of the kings. Historical record indicates that after Romulus a king chosen by the assembly of the people and the Senate (made up of the heads of the most important families) was granted a form of power (**imperium**) that amounted to despotism. The arrival of the Tarquin family may reflect an Etruscan takeover, which was interrupted by the reign of Servius and then thrown off when the last of the kings, Tarquinius Superbus, was banished. That the area of the Forum was drained and paved over and that the first buildings appeared on the Capitoline Hill in the period that corresponds roughly with the arrival of the Tarquins are facts that the archaeologists confirm.

---

1. Summarize the reign of each king in a sentence or two. What overall trends do you find in this period of three centuries?
2. Romans always seemed ambiguous about their kings. What would they find positive and negative about the period of the monarchy?
3. If you had to live in Rome during the monarchy, under which king would you choose to live and why?

VEHICLE SPOTTING

Dum raeda in fossā manēbat, Mārcus et Sextus vehicula exspectābant. Longum erat silentium.

Diū nūllum vehiculum appāret. Tandem Mārcus murmur rotārum audit et procul nūbem pulveris cōnspicit.

Sextus, "Quid est, Mārce? Estne plaustrum?"   5

Mārcus, "Minimē, fatue! Plaustra onera magna ferunt. Tarda igitur sunt. Sed illud vehiculum celeriter appropinquat."

Sextus, "Ita vērō! Praetereā equī illud vehiculum trahunt. Bovēs plaustra trahunt. Fortasse est raeda."

"Nōn est raeda," inquit Mārcus, "nam quattuor rotās habet raeda. Illud vehiculum   10
duās tantum rotās habet."

"Est cisium!" clāmat Sextus. "Ecce, Mārce! Quam celeriter appropinquat! Fortasse est vir praeclārus quī ab urbe Neāpolim iter facit."

"Minimē, Sexte!" respondet Mārcus. "Nōn est vir praeclārus, nam tunicam, nōn togam, gerit. Fortasse est alius tabellārius."   15

Praeterit cisium. Tum nūbem pulveris tantum vident et murmur rotārum audiunt. Tandem silentium.

1 **exspectō, exspectāre,** *to look out for*	**tardus,** *slow*
longus, *long*	**illud,** *that*
3 **diū,** adv., *for a long time*	8 **praetereā,** adv., *besides*
appāreō, appārēre, *to appear*	**bōs, bovis,** m./f., *ox*
rota, -ae, f., *wheel*	9 **fortasse,** adv., *perhaps*
4 **procul,** adv., *in the distance, far off*	10 **quattuor,** *four*
nūbēs, nūbis, gen. pl., **nūbium,** f., *cloud*	11 **duae,** *two*
	tantum, adv., *only*
pulvis, pulveris, m., *dust*	13 Neāpolim, *to Naples*
5 **plaustrum, -ī,** n., *wagon, cart*	16 **praetereō, praeterīre,** irreg., *to go past*
6 **onus, oneris,** n., *load, burden*	

EXERCISE 15a

Go Online
PHSchool.com
Web Code: jfd-0015

Respondē Latīnē:

1. Quid puerī faciēbant ubi raeda in fossā manēbat?
2. Erantne multa vehicula in viā?
3. Quid Mārcus audit et cōnspicit?
4. Cūr vehiculum plaustrum esse nōn potest?
5. Cūr vehiculum raeda esse nōn potest?
6. Quid est?
7. Estne vir praeclārus in cisiō?

FORMS

Nouns: Neuter

Some Latin nouns end with the same letters in the nominative and accusative singular and with the letter *-a* in the nominative and accusative plural. Second declension nouns of this type end with the letters *-um* in the nominative and accusative singular. These are *neuter* nouns. **Neuter** is the Latin word for "neither"; neuter nouns are neither masculine nor feminine (for the concept of gender, see page 34).

Look at the following sentences in which nouns ending with the letters *-um* in the singular and *-a* in the plural are used first as subject and then as direct object:

Baculum Dāvī in vīllā est.	S	*Davus's **stick** is in the farmhouse.*
Dāvus **baculum** habet. (11:8)	DO	*Davus has a **stick**.*
Vēstīgia Getae in silvā sunt.	S	*Geta's **footprints** are in the woods.*
Vēstīgia Getae inveniunt. (12:11)	DO	*They find Geta's **footprints**.*

The words **baculum** and **vēstīgia** are neuter nouns of the 2nd declension. Both the 2nd and the 3rd declensions have neuter nouns:

Number Case	2nd Declension	3rd Declension
Singular		
Nominative	bácul*um*	nómen
Genitive	bácul*ī*	nómin*is*
Dative	bácul*ō*	nómin*ī*
Accusative	bácul*um*	nómen
Ablative	bácul*ō*	nómin*e*
Vocative	bácul*um*	nómen
Plural		
Nominative	bácul*a*	nómin*a*
Genitive	bacul*ṓrum*	nómin*um*
Dative	bácul*īs*	nōmín*ibus*
Accusative	bácul*a*	nómin*a*
Ablative	bácul*īs*	nōmín*ibus*
Vocative	bácul*a*	nómin*a*

Most neuter nouns of the 2nd declension end in *-um* in the nominative and the accusative singular.

The nominative and accusative singular forms of neuter nouns of the 3rd declension, such as **nōmen** and **murmur**, are not predictable, but the other cases are formed by adding the usual 3rd declension endings to the base, which is found by dropping the ending from the genitive singular form.

Remember that the accusative singular of neuter nouns is always the same as the nominative singular and that the nominative and accusative plurals always end in *-a*.

Most 1st declension nouns are feminine. Most 2nd declension nouns are either masculine or neuter. The 3rd declension contains many nouns that are masculine, many that are feminine, and a number of neuter nouns. See the chart on page 136 at the end of this book for examples of nouns of the different genders in each declension.

Examples of neuter nouns are:

2nd Declension
auxilium, -ī, n., *help*
baculum, -ī, n., *stick*
cisium, -ī, n., *light two-wheeled carriage*
cubiculum, -ī, n., *room, bedroom*
olīvētum, -ī, n., *olive grove*
perīculum, -ī, n., *danger*
plaustrum, -ī, n., *wagon, cart*
silentium, -ī, n., *silence*
vehiculum, -ī, n., *vehicle*
vēstīgium, -ī, n., *track, footprint, trace*

3rd Declension
iter, itineris, n., *journey*
murmur, murmuris, n., *murmur, rumble*
nōmen, nōminis, n., *name*
onus, oneris, n., *load*
tempus, temporis, n., *time*

BUILDING THE MEANING

Go Online
PHSchool.com
Web Code: jfd-0015

Nominative, Accusative, or Genitive Plural? How Do You Decide?

At the top of page 114 you saw the words **baculum** and **vēstīgia** used in sentences, first as subjects and then as direct objects. To decide which case is being used, you need to consider the sentence as a whole, just as you have learned to do when other nouns are present that have endings that could be more than one case.

Up to now, the case ending *-a* has indicated a 1st declension nominative singular, e.g., **puella**, but now you can see that if the noun is neuter the ending *-a* could indicate either nominative or accusative plural, e.g., **bacula** or **onera**.

Up to now, the ending *-um* has indicated either a 2nd declension accusative singular of a masculine noun, e.g., **puerum**, or a 3rd declension genitive plural, e.g., **mātrum**, but now you can see that if a noun is 2nd declension and neuter the ending *-um* could indicate either a nominative or accusative singular, e.g., **baculum**.

Note also that the nominative and accusative singular forms of some 3rd declension neuter nouns end with the letters *-us*, e.g., **onus**. You need to know that this is a 3rd declension neuter noun rather than a 2nd declension masculine noun such as **servus**. The word **servus** could only be nominative, while **onus** could be either nominative or accusative.

Now that neuter nouns have been introduced, it is particularly important to note the gender and declension of a noun when you learn vocabulary.

EXERCISE 15b

Read each sentence aloud. Identify each neuter noun and its declension. How can you tell the case of each noun ending in **-a** or **-um**? Translate each sentence:

1. Nūllum vehiculum cōnspicere poterant puerī.
2. Prīnceps magnās vōcēs senātōrum audīre nōlēbat.
3. Nox erat; raeda in fossā immōbilis manēbat; nēmō auxilium ferēbat.
4. Canis lātrābat quod murmur rotārum audiēbat.
5. Sorōrem clāmōrēs frātrum vexābant.
6. Magna onera ferēbant plaustra.
7. Erant multa vehicula in viā; cisium tarda vehicula praeterībat.
8. Magnum onus fert plaustrum.
9. Necesse erat iter Rōmam facere.
10. Servī vēstīgia canum in agrīs inveniunt.
11. Ubi cisium praeterit, est magnum perīculum.
12. Magnum onus nōn fert raeda.

FORMS

Roman Numerals and Latin Numbers

I	**ūnus, -a, -um,** *one*	VIII	**octō,** *eight*
II	**duo, -ae, -o,** *two*	IX	**novem,** *nine*
III	**trēs, trēs, tria,** *three*	X	**decem,** *ten*
IV	**quattuor,** *four*	L	**quīnquāgintā,** *fifty*
V	**quīnque,** *five*	C	**centum,** *a hundred*
VI	**sex,** *six*	D	**quīngentī, -ae, -a,** *five hundred*
VII	**septem,** *seven*	M	**mīlle,** *a thousand*

The words above are adjectives. The masculine, feminine, and neuter endings or forms are given for the numbers one, two, three, and five hundred. The others never change their form. Here are forms for **ūnus, duo,** and **trēs:**

Case	Masc.	Fem.	Neut.	Masc.	Fem.	Neut.	Masc.	Fem.	Neut.
Nom.	ū́n**us**	ū́na	ū́n**um**	dúo	dúae	dúo	trēs	trēs	tr**ía**
Gen.	ūn**ī́us**	ūn**ī́us**	ūn**ī́us**	du**ṓrum**	du**ā́rum**	du**ṓrum**	tr**íum**	tr**íum**	tr**íum**
Dat.	ū́n**ī**	ū́n**ī**	ū́n**ī**	du**ṓbus**	du**ā́bus**	du**ṓbus**	tr**íbus**	tr**íbus**	tr**íbus**
Acc.	ū́n**um**	ū́n**am**	ū́n**um**	dúo**s**	dúā**s**	dúo	trēs	trēs	tr**ía**
Abl.	ū́n**ō**	ū́n**ā**	ū́n**ō**	du**ṓbus**	du**ā́bus**	du**ṓbus**	tr**íbus**	tr**íbus**	tr**íbus**

In the stories, you have met the following other adjectives that have **-īus** in the genitive singular and **-ī** in the dative singular: **alius, -a, -ud,** *another, other* (10); **alter, altera, alterum,** *second, one (of two), the other (of two), another,* (1); **nūllus, -a, -um,** *no, not any* (9); and **sōlus, -a, -um,** *alone* (3).

All roads to Rome radiated from the center of the city, a point marked by the Emperor Augustus with the *mīliārium aureum*, a gilded, inscribed bronze milestone. Shown here are peoples of the world who came to Rome, circling the *mīliārium aureum*.

Seventeenth-century European engraving, artist unknown

EXERCISE 15c

Answer the questions by supplying the Latin words for the appropriate numbers, read aloud, and translate:

1. Quot rotās raeda habet? _____ rotās raeda habet.
2. Quot rotās plaustrum habet? _____ rotās plaustrum habet.
3. Quot rotās cisium habet? _____ rotās cisium habet.
4. Quot equī raedam trahunt? _____ equī raedam trahunt.
5. Quot bovēs plaustrum trahunt? _____ bovēs plaustrum trahunt.
6. Quot līberōs in raedā vidēs? In raedā _____ puellam et _____ puerōs videō.
7. Quot parentēs in raedā vidēs? _____ parentēs in raedā videō.
8. Quot līberī cum quot parentibus Rōmam raedā iter faciēbant?
   _____ puella et _____ puerī cum _____ parentibus Rōmam raedā iter faciēbant.

   Quot...? *How many...?*

EXERCISE 15d

Respondē Latīnē:

1. Sī duo puerī et octō puellae iter faciunt, quot līberī iter faciunt?
2. Sī duae puellae et trēs puerī iter faciunt, quot līberī iter faciunt?
3. Sī sex parentēs et trēs puellae iter faciunt, quot hominēs iter faciunt?
4. Sī quīnque parentēs et trēs puerī iter faciunt, quot hominēs iter faciunt?
5. Sī quattuor puerī et sex puellae iter faciunt, quot līberī iter faciunt?
6. Sī quattuor puellae et quīnque puerī iter faciunt, quot līberī iter faciunt?
7. Sī quattuor puellae et trēs puerī iter faciunt, quot līberī iter faciunt?

   hominēs, hominum, m. pl., *people*

WHY IS SEXTUS A PEST?

Iam nōna hōra erat. Adhūc immōbilis in fossā haerēbat raeda. Sed nihil facere Sextum taedēbat, nam puer strēnuus erat. Subitō igitur ad raedam currit et cistam aperit. Tum ē cistā pilam extrahit.

"Vīsne pilā lūdere, Mārce?" clāmat. Pilam ad Mārcum statim iacit. Mārcus eam excipit et ad Sextum mittit. Identidem puerī pilam iaciēbant, alter ad alterum. Tum 5 Sextus, quī semper Cornēliam vexāre vult, per iocum pilam iacit et Cornēliam ferit.

Statim īrāta Cornēlia ad mātrem sē vertit et, "Cūr mē semper vexat Sextus, māter?" clāmat. "Cūr pilam in mē iacit? Quam molestus puer est Sextus!"

"Venī ad mē, cārissima," respondet māter et fīliam complexū tenet. "Sextus tē ferīre in animō nōn habēbat. Est puer strēnuus, est puer temerārius, nōn tamen est puer 10 scelestus."

"Sed cūr Sextus apud nōs habitat?" rogat Cornēlia, quae adhūc īrāta est. "Cūr pater Sextī eum ad nōs mittit?"

(continued)

1 nōnus, *ninth*
2 Sextum taedēbat, *it bored Sextus*
3 **aperiō, aperīre,** *to open*
   pila, -ae, f., *ball*
4 Vīsne…? *Do you want…?*
   lūdō, lūdere, *to play*
      pilā lūdere, *to play ball*
   eam, *her, it*
5 **excipiō, excipere,** *to welcome, receive, catch*

alter…alterum, *the one…the other*
6 **iocus, -ī,** m., *joke, prank*
   per iocum, *as a prank*
   feriō, ferīre, *to hit, strike*
7 **vertō, vertere,** *to turn*
9 cārissima, *dearest*
10 **animus, -ī,** m., *mind*
   in animō habēre, *to intend*
12 **apud,** prep. + acc., *at the house of, with*

EXERCISE 16a

Go Online
PHSchool.com
Web Code: jfd-0016

Respondē Latīnē:

1. Cūr nihil facere Sextum taedēbat?
2. Quid facit Sextus?
3. Quid faciēbant puerī?

4. Cūr est Cornēlia īrāta?
5. Habēbatne Sextus in animō Cornēliam ferīre?
6. Quālis puer est Sextus?

"Pater Sextī ad Asiam iter facit. Quod pater abest, necesse erat Sextum in Italiā relinquere. Itaque, quod pater Sextī hospes patris tuī est, Sextus apud nōs manet." 15

"Quid tamen dē mātre Sextī?" rogat filia. "Cūr illa fīlium nōn cūrat?"

"Ēheu!" respondet Aurēlia. "Māter Sextī, ut scīs, iam mortua est. Mātrem nōn habet Sextus." Tacēbat Cornēlia, nōn iam īrā commōta.

Eō ipsō tempore tamen Sextus, "Vīsne nōbīscum lūdere, Cornēlia?" exclāmat. "Quamquam tū es puella, pilam iacere fortasse potes." Dum clāmābat, iam rīdēbat et 20 effugiēbat. Iterum īrāta Cornēlia, "Abī, moleste puer!" clāmat. "Pilā lūdere nōlō."

15 **relinquō, relinquere,** *to leave behind*
   itaque, adv., *and so, therefore*
   hospes, hospitis, m./f., *host, guest, friend*
16 **dē,** prep. + abl., *down from, concerning, about*

illa, *she*
17 **ut,** conj., *as*
   sciō, scīre, *to know*
   mortuus, -a, -um, *dead*
19 nōbīscum = cum nōbīs, *with us*

Respondē Latīnē:

7. Cūr Sextus cum Cornēliīs habitat?
8. Cūr māter Sextī fīlium nōn cūrat?
9. Vultne Cornēlia pilā lūdere?

BUILDING THE MEANING

Go Online
PHSchool.com
Web Code: jfd-0016

Nouns and Adjectives: Agreement I

In Chapter 6, you learned the general principle that an adjective always agrees with the noun it describes or modifies. Adjective agreement must be considered from three points of view:

1. The adjective must be the same *gender* as the noun it modifies:
   magn**us** canis   (masculine)
   magn**a** vōx   (feminine)
   magn**um** iter   (neuter)

2. The adjective must be the same *case* as the noun it modifies:
   magn**us** canis   (nominative)
   magn**ī** canis   (genitive)
   magn**um** canem   (accusative)
   magn**ō** cane   (ablative)

3. The adjective must be the same *number* (singular or plural) as the noun it modifies:

magn*us* canis	(singular)	magn*ī* canēs	(plural)
magn*a* vōx	(singular)	magn*ae* vōcēs	(plural)
magn*um* iter	(singular)	magn*a* itinera	(plural)

The fact that adjectives must agree with their nouns does *not* mean that the adjective and noun will always have identical endings, as the examples above show. Most of the adjectives you have met use the same endings as the 2nd declension masculine noun **servus** when they modify masculine nouns; they use the same endings as the 1st declension noun **puella** when they modify feminine nouns; and they use the same endings as the 2nd declension neuter noun **baculum** when they modify neuter nouns. For this reason they are referred to as *1st and 2nd declension adjectives*. Here is a complete chart of the 1st and 2nd declension adjective **magnus, magna, magnum**. Note the order of the columns in the chart: masculine (2nd), feminine (1st), neuter (2nd):

Number Case	1st and 2nd Declensions		
	Masc.	**Fem.**	**Neut.**
Singular			
Nominative	mágn*us*	mágn*a*	mágn*um*
Genitive	mágn*ī*	mágn*ae*	mágn*ī*
Dative	mágn*ō*	mágn*ae*	mágn*ō*
Accusative	mágn*um*	mágn*am*	mágn*um*
Ablative	mágn*ō*	mágn*ā*	mágn*ō*
Vocative	mágn*e*	mágn*a*	mágn*um*
Plural			
Nominative	mágn*ī*	mágn*ae*	mágn*a*
Genitive	magn*órum*	magn*árum*	magn*órum*
Dative	mágn*īs*	mágn*īs*	mágn*īs*
Accusative	mágn*ōs*	mágn*ās*	mágn*a*
Ablative	mágn*īs*	mágn*īs*	mágn*īs*
Vocative	mágn*ī*	mágn*ae*	mágn*a*

Look at the following example:

Cum senātōr*e* Rōmān*ō* iter facit.

In this sentence **Rōmānō** is masculine ablative singular in agreement with **senātōre**. The endings are different since the noun belongs to the 3rd declension, while the adjective uses 1st and 2nd declension endings (2nd declension for masculine, as here). Sometimes, of course, the endings may be the same, when the adjective and noun belong to the same declension:

Cum vir*ō* Rōmān*ō* iter facit.   Cum fēmin*ā* Rōmān*ā* iter facit.

SUMMARY: Adjectives agree with the nouns they describe in *gender*, *case*, and *number*. The adjective and the noun it modifies may belong to different declensions and end with different letters.

In future vocabulary lists, 1st and 2nd declension adjectives will be given as follows: **magnus, -a, -um**, *big, great, large, loud (voice, laugh)*, showing the masculine nominative singular form and the endings of the feminine and neuter nominative singular forms.

EXERCISE 16b

For each noun below, first identify the declension of the noun, then tell what gender, case, and number it is, and finally give the proper form of the adjective **bonus, -a, -um** to modify the noun:

1. cubiculī
2. filiārum
3. clāmōrem
4. vōcum
5. itinere
6. servīs
7. auxilium (3 possibilities)
8. puellam
9. nōminis
10. artem
11. patrēs (3 possibilities)
12. cīvis (6 possibilities)

EXERCISE 16c

Read each sentence aloud. Identify all noun-adjective pairs. Check your identification by noting the gender, case, and number of both items in each pair. Then translate:

1. Aliī servī equōs dominī in viam dūcēbant, aliī ē vīllā currēbant et magnās cistās in raedam pōnēbant.
2. Ubi Cornēlius multās epistulās scrībit, nēmō eum impedit.
3. Sī līberōrum magnae vōcēs patrem vexant, Aurēlia puerōs strēnuōs in hortum mittit.
4. Puellārum nōmina vocat ancilla nova; sed strēnuae puellae magnam vōcem ancillae nōn audiunt.
5. Plaustrum duās habet rotās; in plaustra onera magna rūsticī pōnunt; plaustra bovēs tardī per viās in magnam urbem nocte trahunt.
6. Magnum numerum servōrum Cornēlius in vīneā vīcīnā spectābat.
7. Cūnctī servī spectābant Getam, quī in rāmīs arboris dormiēbat.

vocō, vocāre, *to call*   **novus, -a, -um,** *new*

EXERCISE 16d

Make the adjectives in parentheses agree with the nouns (if necessary, use the Latin to English vocabulary list at the end of the book to find the gender of the nouns):

1. aestātem (calidus)
2. nocte (frīgidus)
3. sorōribus (bonus)
4. urbis (magnus)
5. ars (novus)
6. nōminum (alius)
7. onera (magnus)
8. viātōrēs (tardus) (2 possibilities)
9. bovēs (tardus) (4 possibilities)
10. fragōris (magnus)

Word Study IV

Numbers

The Latin words for numbers provide English with a great many words. For example, the English word *unite* (to bring together as *one*) comes from the Latin number **ūnus**. The English word *duet* (music for *two* performers) is derived from **duo** in Latin, and *triple* (*three* fold) traces its ancestry to the Latin **trēs**.

EXERCISE 1

Match these English words with their meanings:

1. sextet
2. unique
3. decimate
4. quadrant
5. duplex
6. septuagenarians
7. octagon
8. triad
9. quintuplets
10. century

a. five babies born together
b. an eight-sided figure
c. one-of-a-kind, without equal
d. people in their seventies
e. to destroy one tenth of
f. a set of three
g. one fourth of a circle
h. a period of 100 years
i. a group of six
j. a two-family house or an apartment on two levels

The Roman Number System

The origin of Roman numerals from one to ten is in the human hand. The Roman numeral I is one finger held up; the numeral II is two fingers, and so on. The numeral V comes from the v-shape between the thumb and the other four fingers pressed together, and it therefore represents five. When two V's are placed with their points touching, the numeral X is formed, representing ten. A limited number of letters were used by the Romans to express numerals: 1 = 1, V = 5, X = 10, L = 50, C = 100, D = 500, and M = 1000. All Roman numerals are based on these.

The number system of the Romans may seem awkward compared with the Arabic system we use today. As Roman numerals grew larger, they became increasingly hard to read. Although no longer used in mathematics, Roman numerals are still part of our everyday experience: on the face of a clock, in the chapter headings of our books, and in writing the year of an important date.

Here are some rules to remember about Roman numerals:

1. A numeral followed by a smaller numeral represents addition: VI = 5 + 1 = 6.
2. A numeral followed by a larger numeral represents subtraction: IV = 5 - 1 = 4.
3. A smaller numeral between two larger numerals is subtracted from the second of the larger numerals: MCM = 1000 + (1000 - 100) = 1900.

**Roman milestone
of A.D. 217/218**
Trentino, Alto Adige

EXERCISE 2

Give the following in Arabic numerals:

1. XXI	6. XXXIV
2. DC	7. LXXXVIII
3. XL	8. MDLXXIII
4. LVII	9. MCMXLVI
5. XIX	10. MDCCCLXIV

EXERCISE 3

Give the following in Roman numerals:

1. your age
2. the year of our story, A.D. 80
3. the current year
4. the year Rome was founded, 753 B.C.
5. your age in 25 years time

EXERCISE 4

Find five examples of Roman numerals in use in your environment.

EXERCISE 5

In Chapter 19 you will read the Roman poet Horace's account of his journey from Rome to Brundisium. On page 125 is a map showing the route of his journey, along with his itinerary indicating the distances in Roman numerals. Convert each Roman numeral into its corresponding Arabic numeral, and give the Roman numeral for the total miles that Horace traveled.

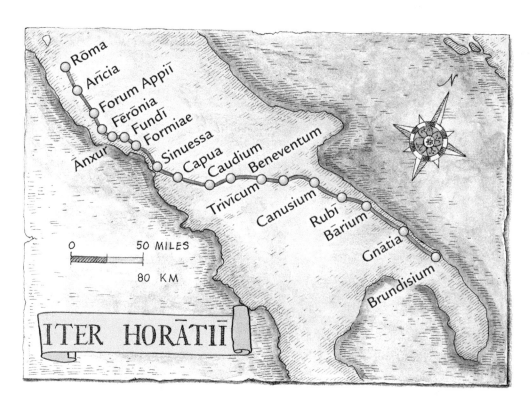

Stage of Journey	Distance
Day 1: Rome to Aricia	XV miles
Day 2: Aricia to Forum Appii	XXIII miles
Day 3: Canal boat to Feronia	XV miles
Feronia to Anxur	IV miles
Anxur to Fundi	XIII miles
Fundi to Formiae	XV miles
Day 4: Formiae to Sinuessa	XXIV miles
Day 5: Sinuessa to Capua	XXXV miles
Capua to Caudium	XX miles
Day 6: Caudium to Beneventum	XV miles
Day 7: Beneventum to Trivicum	XXIII miles
Day 8: By coach to unnamed town	XXVIII miles
Day 9: To Canusium	XXX miles
Canusium to Rubi	XXV miles
Day 10: Rubi to Barium	XXIII miles
Day 11: Barium to Gnatia	XXX miles
Day 12: Gnatia to Brundisium	XXXVIII miles

DO WE STAY AT AN INN?

Erat ūndecima hōra. Raeda adhūc in fossā manēbat quod raedārius eam movēre nōn poterat. Aurēlia sollicita erat; Cornēlia lacrimābat; etiam puerī perīcula iam timēbant; Cornēlius in viā stābat sollicitus et caelum spectābat quod iam advesperāscēbat.

Tandem Eucleidēs, "Vidēsne illud aedificium, domine?" inquit.

"Videō," Cornēlius respondet. "Quid est?" 5

"Caupōna est. Vīsne igitur ibi pernoctāre, domine?"

Clāmat Aurēlia, "Ō mē miseram! Caupōnās nōn amō. Saepe ibi perīcula sunt magna. Fortasse caupō aliōs equōs habet. Fortasse equī caupōnis raedam ē fossā extrahere possunt. In caupōnā pernoctāre timeō."

"Cūr timēs, mea domina?" Eucleidēs rogat. "Nūllum est perīculum. Nōn omnēs 10 caupōnae sunt perīculōsae. Nōn omnēs caupōnēs sunt scelestī. Ille caupō est amīcus meus. Graecus est et vir bonus."

Tum Aurēlia, "Cornēlius est senātor Rōmānus. Senātōrēs Rōmānī in caupōnīs nōn pernoctant."

Cornēlius tamen, "Quid facere possumus?" inquit. "Hīc in Viā Appiā pernoctāre nōn 15 possumus. Nūlla vehicula iam appārent quod advesperāscit. Est nūllum auxilium. Illa caupōna nōn procul abest. Necesse est igitur ad caupōnam īre. Agite, puerī!"

Itaque, dum Eucleidēs Cornēliōs ad caupōnam dūcēbat, raedārius sōlus in viā manēbat; raedam et equōs custōdiēbat.

1 ūndecimus, -a, -um, *eleventh*
3 **caelum, -ī,** n., *sky*
 advesperāscit, advesperāscere, *it gets dark*
4 **aedificium, -ī,** n., *building*
6 **caupōna, -ae,** f., *inn*

 pernoctō, pernoctāre, *to spend the night*
8 **caupō, caupōnis,** m., *innkeeper*
11 **perīculōsus, -a, -um,** *dangerous*
12 Graecus, -a, -um, *Greek*
19 **custōdiō, custōdīre,** *to guard*

EXERCISE 17a

Respondē Latīnē:

1. Cūr raeda in fossā manēbat?
2. Cūr Cornēlius sollicitus erat?
3. Quid videt Eucleidēs?
4. Ubi pernoctāre possunt?
5. Cūr Aurēlia in caupōnā pernoctāre nōn vult?
6. Ubi Cornēliī pernoctāre nōn possunt?
7. Quis raedam et equōs custōdiēbat?

Go Online
PHSchool.com
Web Code: jfd-0017

FORMS

Verbs: Regular Verbs (Review)

Most Latin verbs are regular and belong to one of four conjugations. Review the present and imperfect forms of such verbs, as given on page 271 of the Forms section at the end of this book. Practice by giving the present and imperfect and imperatives of the following verbs: **amō, amāre; iubeō, iubēre; currō, currere; faciō, facere;** and **dormiō, dormīre**.

Verbs: Irregular Verbs II

Some verbs are irregular, like **sum, esse** and its compounds (see page 108). Four other common irregular verbs, like **sum** and its compounds, do not belong to any one of the four conjugations: **volō, velle,** *to wish, want, be willing;* **nōlō** (= **nōn volō**), **nōlle,** *not to wish, not to want, to be unwilling;* **ferō, ferre,** *to bring, carry;* and **eō, īre,** *to go.* You will notice that these irregular verbs have the same personal endings as the regular verbs:

The Present Tense				
Infinitive	vélle	nőlle	férre	íre
Imperative	—	nőlī	fer	ī
	—	nőlíte	férte	íte
Singular 1	vólō	nőlō	férō	éō
2	vīs	nōn vīs	fers	īs
3	vult	nōn vult	fert	it
Plural 1	vólumus	nőlumus	férimus	ímus
2	vúltis	nōn vúltis	fértis	ítis
3	vólunt	nőlunt	férunt	éunt

The Imperfect Tense				
Singular 1	volébam	nōlébam	ferébam	íbam
2	volébās	nōlébās	ferébās	íbās
3	volébat	nōlébat	ferébat	íbat
Plural 1	volēbámus	nōlēbámus	ferēbámus	ībámus
2	volēbátis	nōlēbátis	ferēbátis	ībátis
3	volébant	nōlébant	ferébant	íbant

Be sure to learn these forms thoroughly.

EXERCISE 17b

Read aloud and translate:

1. In fossam dēscendere nōlō.
2. Plaustrum onus fert.
3. Cornēliī et Eucleidēs ad caupōnam eunt.
4. Syrus raedam ē fossā extrahere vult.
5. Cistās ad raedam ferimus.
6. Cum amīcīs Rōmam eō.

7. Aurēlia in caupōnā pernoctāre nōn vult.
8. Ī, fatue!
9. Servī cistās ferunt.
10. Ubi pernoctāre vīs, domine?
11. Nōlī in caupōnam īre, Cornēlia!
12. Fer aquam, serve!

EXERCISE 17c

Read each question aloud. Then give an answer in a complete sentence in Latin:

1. Ubi Sextus manēbat?
2. Unde Cornēliī veniunt?
3. Cūr Rōmam īre nōn poterant?
4. Quid fers, Dāve?
5. Quid faciēbātis, servī?
6. Erātisne diū in fossā?
7. Quō Cornēliī īre volunt?
8. Quid puellae in agrīs faciēbant?
9. Quid Dāvus servōs et ancillās facere iubēbat?
10. Poterāsne clāmāre?
11. Quō ītis, Cornēliī?
12. Quid ferēbās, Dāve?
13. Quid facitis, servī?
14. Quid in viā vidēs, Sexte?
15. Ubi haeret raeda?
16. Cūr in viā pernoctāre nōn vultis?
17. Quō ībant Cornēliī?
18. Cūr ad urbem īre Cornēlia nōn vult?
19. Unde veniēbās, Cornēlia?
20. Scelestusne sum?
21. Quō Syrus equōs dūcit?
22. Cūr equī īre nōn possunt?
23. Quid nōn procul aberat?
24. Cūr in caupōnā pernoctāre nōlēbātis?

EXERCISE 17d

Give the Latin for the following (use irregular verbs):

1. Carry the chests to the inn, slaves!
2. Marcus, why are you carrying Sextus's chest?
3. We do not wish to spend the night in an inn.
4. We were going to Rome.
5. Sextus wants to see the great Roman buildings.
6. Do you wish to see the buildings, Marcus?
7. We are going to Rome today.
8. The slow wagon is carrying a large load.
9. All the Roman senators are going to the city.
10. I am going to my country house.

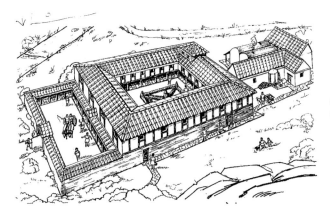

A Roman country inn

**Bedroom (*cubiculum*) in the *vīlla rūstica* of P. Fannius Synistor at Boscoreale near Pompeii.
We use this villa at Boscoreale as a model for the villa of the Cornelii at Baiae.**
Fresco, second style ca. 40–30 B.C.

Review III: Chapters 13–17

Web Code: jfd-0017

Exercise IIIa: Present and Imperfect of Regular and Irregular Verbs

pp. 98, 106–107, 108, 128

In each sentence below supply the appropriate form of each of the following verbs or verbal phrases, first in the present and then in the imperfect tense. Read aloud and translate each sentence you make:

cūrō	cōnspiciō	portāre volō
moveō	custōdiō	portāre nōlō
extrahō	portāre possum	ferō

1. Ego cistam _____.
2. Tū cistam _____.
3. Servus cistam _____.
4. Nōs cistam _____.
5. Vōs cistam _____.
6. Servī cistam _____.

In each sentence below, supply the appropriate form of the verb **eō** first in the present and then in the imperfect tense. Translate each sentence you make:

1. Ego Rōmam _____.
2. Tū Rōmam _____.
3. Cornēlius Rōmam _____.
4. Nōs Rōmam _____.
5. Vōs Rōmam _____.
6. Cornēliī Rōmam _____.

Exercise IIIb: Neuter Nouns

pp. 114–115

Change the nouns and adjectives in italics to plural, make any other necessary changes, read aloud, and translate:

1. Puerī in *cubiculō* dormiēbant.
2. Servus *onus magnum* portat.
3. Sextus *murmur* rōtārum in viā audiēbat.
4. Cornēliī nōn in *cisiō* iter faciēbant.
5. *Magnum perīculum* in viīs est.
6. Cornēlius servōs *baculō* verberābat.
7. Senātor ad urbem *iter* facit.
8. *Raeda* est *vehiculum Rōmānum*.
9. *Rūsticus* in *plaustrō* dormit.
10. *Rōta cisiī īnfirma* erat.

Exercise IIIc: Numbers

pp. 116, 123

Read the following sentences aloud, filling in the blanks as you go with Latin words for the appropriate numbers:

1. Quot fīliōs habet Cornēlius? Cornēlius _____ fīlium habet.
2. Quot fīliās habet Cornēlius? Cornēlius _____ fīliam habet.
3. Numerus līberōrum Cornēliī est _____.
4. Quot pedēs habet lupus? Lupus _____ pedēs habet.
5. Quot līberī ad urbem iter faciunt? _____ līberī ad urbem iter faciunt.

(continued)

6. Quot rotās habent raeda et cisium? Raeda et cisium _____ rotās habent.
7. Quot pedēs habent duo lupī? Duo lupī habent _____ pedēs.
8. Quot nōmina habet Cornēlius? Cornēlius _____ nōmina habet.
9. Quot nōmina habet Cornēlia? Cornēlia _____ nōmen habet.
10. Quot pedēs habent trēs puerī? Trēs puerī _____ pedēs habent.

Exercise IIId: Nouns and Cases REVIEW p. 81

Select the correct word, read the sentence aloud, and translate it:

1. In agrīs errābant _____.   puerōs/puerī/puerōrum
2. Cornēlius multōs _____ habēbat.   canēs/servum/ancillās/amīcī
3. Quid facit _____?   Aurēliam/Aurēlia/Aurēliae
4. Rūsticī _____ baculīs excitant.   canis/bovēs/equus
5. Quam molesta est _____!   Sextus/puellae/Flāvia/Cornēliam
6. Sub arborum rāmīs dormit _____.   cīvēs/servus/rūsticōs
7. Canēs lātrantēs _____ timēbant.   puer/puerī/puella
8. In agrīs _____ sunt multae arborēs.   Cornēliī/vīllā/vīneam
9. Ancillae līberōrum _____ cūrābant.   tunica/tunicae/canis/cistās
10. _____ novās _____ induere   puella/puellae/tunica/tunicās
    volunt.

Exercise IIIe: Agreement of Adjectives and Nouns REVIEW pp. 120–121

For each adjective below, select the noun or nouns that are in the correct
gender, case, and number for the adjective to modify them. Explain your
choices:

1. magna   nox, onera, fragore, rotā
2. magnīs   nocte, oneribus, servīs, fēminās, rotīs
3. magnae   dominī, rotae, onerī, vōcis
4. magnōs   vōcēs, fragōrēs, fīliōs, pedēs
5. magnum   onus, vōcum, baculum, cistam

Exercise IIIf: Adverbs pp. 100–101

Often nouns and adverbs have the same endings. Identify the adverbs in the following sets of words. Give the meaning of each adverb:

1. fortasse
   frātre
   saepe
   sorōre

2. fossā
   frūstrā
   intereā
   pictūrā
   praetereā

3. etiam
   iam
   iānuam

4. iānitōrem
   identidem
   tandem

5. iter
   iterum

6. deinde
   mātre
   nōmine

7. nōndum
   numerum

8. rāmō
   rārō
   silentiō
   subitō

Exercise IIIg: Adverbs from 1st and 2nd Declension Adjectives   pp. 100–101

Make adverbs from the following adjectives. Give the meanings of the adverbs:

1. temerārius, -a, -um
2. scelestus, -a, -um
3. praeclārus, -a, -um
4. perīculōsus, -a, -um
5. novus, -a, -um
6. strēnuus, -a, -um
7. miser, misera, miserum
8. tacitus, -a, -um
9. lentus, -a, -um
10. īrātus, -a, -um

Exercise IIIh: Reading Comprehension

Read the following passage and answer the questions with full sentences in Latin:

ONE HERO WINS A WAR

Ubi Tullus Hostilius, rēx tertius, Rōmānōs regēbat, pugnābant Rōmānī cum cīvibus Albae Longae, urbis quae nōn procul aberat. Pugnāre tamen volēbant neque Rōmānī neque Albānī, nam multī Rōmānī aut amīcōs aut propinquōs in urbe Albā Longā habēbant. Itaque Rōmānī cōnsilium capiunt et nūntiōs ad Albānōs mittunt. 5

Nūntiī, "Nōn necesse est," inquiunt, "cūnctīs Rōmānīs cum cūnctīs Albānīs pugnāre. Nōs inter mīlitēs nostrōs frātrēs habēmus trigeminōs, nōmine Horātiōs. Vōs quoque inter mīlitēs vestrōs frātrēs habētis trigeminōs, nōmine Cūriātiōs. Sī vultis, hī frātrēs cum illīs pugnābunt, et proeliī victōrēs victōriam bellī prō patriā suā reportābunt." 10

Hoc cōnsilium Albānōs dēlectat. Frātrēs in proelium festīnant. Ferōciter pugnant Horātiī Cūriātiīque. Ūnus ē Cūriātiīs vulnus accipit, tum alter, deinde tertius. Cūriātiī tamen duōs ē Horātiīs necant. Ūnus Horātius contrā trēs Cūriātiōs vulnerātōs stat, sōlus sed incolumis. Horātius tamen nōn timet sed cōnsilium capit. 15

Ex illō locō iam currit Horātius et ā Cūriātiīs effugit. Cūriātiī Horātium petunt sed, quod vulnerātī sunt, magnīs intervallīs currunt. Itaque, ubi ūnus Cūriātius frātrēs praeterit, Horātius sē vertit et eum necat. Iterum effugit Horātius; iterum sē vertit et ūnum ē Cūriātiīs necat. Hōc modō omnēs trēs Cūriātiōs necat Horātius ūnus. Victor est Horātius et victōriam bellī habent Rōmānī. 20

1 rēx, rēgis, m., *king*
   tertius, -a, -um, *third*
   regō, regere, *to rule*
   pugnō, pugnāre, *to fight*
3 aut…aut, conj., *either…or*
   propinquus, -ī, m., *relative*
4 cōnsilium, -ī, n., *plan*
      cōnsilium capere, *to form a plan*
6 cūnctīs Rōmānīs, *for all the Romans*
7 inter, prep. + acc., *between, among*
   mīles, mīlitis, m., *soldier*
   trigeminus, -a, -um, *triplet*
8 vester, vestra, vestrum, *your*
9 hī…illīs, *these…those*
   pugnābunt, *(they) will fight*
   proelium, -ī, n., *fight, battle*

victor, victōris, m., *conqueror, victor*
bellum, -ī, n., *war*
prō, prep. + abl., *for, on behalf of*
patria, -ae, f., *nation, native land*
10 reportābunt, *(they) will bring back*
11 dēlectō, dēlectāre, *to please*
12 -que, enclitic conj., *and*
    ē Cūriātiīs, *of the Curiatii*
    vulnus, vulneris, n., *wound*
    accipiō, accipere, *to accept, receive*
13 necō, necāre, *to kill*
    contrā, prep. + acc., *against*
14 vulnerātus, -a, -um, *wounded*
17 magnīs intervallīs, *with big gaps*
       between them
19 hōc modō, *in this way*

1. With whom were the Romans fighting?
2. Were the Romans and Albans eager to fight?
3. Why or why not?
4. What do the Romans do before joining battle?
5. Whom do the Romans have among their soldiers?
6. Whom do the Albans have?
7. How do the Horatii and Curiatii fight?
8. Who receive wounds?
9. Who kills whom?
10. What does the surviving Horatius do when he forms a plan?
11. Why do the Curiatii seek Horatius with big gaps between them?
12. What does Horatius do when one of the Curiatii runs ahead of another?
13. How many Curiatii does Horatius kill?
14. Who is the winner?

Exercise IIIi: Identification of Forms

In the passage on page 134, identify the following:

1. Five imperfect verb forms.
2. Four neuter nouns.
3. Four adverbs.
4. All examples of the Latin words for "one," "two," and "three."
5. Two prepositional phrases using the accusative case and two using the ablative case.

Tradition identifies this tomb as that of the legendary Horatii and Curiatii brothers.
Albano Laziale, Italy, first half of first century B.C.

FORMS

The following charts show the forms of typical Latin nouns, adjectives, pronouns, and verbs in the cases and tenses presented in this book. As an aid in pronunciation, markings of long vowels and of accents are included.

I. Nouns

Number Case	1st Declension Fem.	2nd Declension Masc.	Masc.	Masc.	Neut.	3rd Declension Masc.	Fem.	Neut.
Singular								
Nominative	puélla	sérvus	púer	áger	báculum	páter	vōx	nōmen
Genitive	puéllae	sérvī	púerī	ágrī	báculī	pátris	vōcis	nōminis
Dative	puéllae	sérvō	púerō	ágrō	báculō	pátrī	vōcī	nōminī
Accusative	puéllam	sérvum	púerum	ágrum	báculum	pátrem	vōcem	nōmen
Ablative	puéllā	sérvō	púerō	ágrō	báculō	pátre	vōce	nōmine
Vocative	puélla	sérve	púer	áger	báculum	páter	vōx	nōmen
Plural								
Nominative	puéllae	sérvī	púerī	ágrī	bácula	pátrēs	vōcēs	nōmina
Genitive	puellārum	servōrum	puerōrum	agrōrum	baculōrum	pátrum	vōcum	nōminum
Dative	puéllīs	sérvīs	púerīs	ágrīs	báculīs	pátribus	vōcibus	nōmínibus
Accusative	puéllās	sérvōs	púerōs	ágrōs	bácula	pátrēs	vōcēs	nōmina
Ablative	puéllīs	sérvīs	púerīs	ágrīs	báculīs	pátribus	vōcibus	nōmínibus
Vocative	puéllae	sérvī	púerī	ágrī	bácula	pátrēs	vōcēs	nōmina

II. Adjectives

Number Case	1st and 2nd Declensions Masc.	Fem.	Neut.	3rd Declension Masc.	Fem.	Neut.
Singular						
Nominative	mágnus	mágna	mágnum	ómnis	ómnis	ómne
Genitive	mágnī	mágnae	mágnī	ómnis	ómnis	ómnis
Dative	mágnō	mágnae	mágnō	ómnī	ómnī	ómnī
Accusative	mágnum	mágnam	mágnum	ómnem	ómnem	ómne
Ablative	mágnō	mágnā	mágnō	ómnī	ómnī	ómnī
Vocative	mágne	mágna	mágnum	ómnis	ómnis	ómne
Plural						
Nominative	mágnī	mágnae	mágna	ómnēs	ómnēs	ómnia
Genitive	magnōrum	magnārum	magnōrum	ómnium	ómnium	ómnium
Dative	mágnīs	mágnīs	mágnīs	ómnibus	ómnibus	ómnibus
Accusative	mágnōs	mágnās	mágna	ómnēs	ómnēs	ómnia
Ablative	mágnīs	mágnīs	mágnīs	ómnibus	ómnibus	ómnibus
Vocative	mágnī	mágnae	mágna	ómnēs	ómnēs	ómnia

III. Numbers

Case	Masc.	Fem.	Neut.	Masc.	Fem.	Neut.	Masc.	Fem.	Neut.
Nominative	únus	úna	únum	dúo	dúae	dúo	trēs	trēs	tría
Genitive	ūníus	ūníus	ūníus	duórum	duárum	duórum	tríum	tríum	tríum
Dative	únī	únī	únī	duóbus	duábus	duóbus	tríbus	tríbus	tríbus
Accusative	únum	únam	únum	dúōs	dúās	dúo	trēs	trēs	tría
Ablative	únō	únā	únō	duóbus	duábus	duóbus	tríbus	tríbus	tríbus

IV. Personal Pronouns

Case	1st	2nd	3rd Masc.	3rd Fem.	3rd Neut.	1st (Pl)	2nd (Pl)	3rd Masc.	3rd Fem.	3rd Neut.
				Singular					Plural	
Nominative	égo	tū	is	éa	id	nōs	vōs	éī	éae	éa
Genitive	méī	túī	éius	éius	éius	nóstrī / nóstrum	véstrī / véstrum	eórum	eárum	eórum
Dative	míhi	tíbi	éī	éī	éī	nốbīs	vốbīs	éīs	éīs	éīs
Accusative	mē	tē	éum	éam	id	nōs	vōs	éōs	éās	éa
Ablative	mē	tē	éō	éā	éō	nốbīs	vốbīs	éīs	éīs	éīs

V. Relative Pronoun

Case	Masc. (Sg)	Fem. (Sg)	Neut. (Sg)	Masc. (Pl)	Fem. (Pl)	Neut. (Pl)
Nominative	quī	quae	quod	quī	quae	quae
Genitive	cúius	cúius	cúius	quórum	quárum	quórum
Dative	cui	cui	cui	quíbus	quíbus	quíbus
Accusative	quem	quam	quod	quōs	quās	quae
Ablative	quō	quā	quō	quíbus	quíbus	quíbus

VI. Interrogative Pronoun

Number / Case	Masc. (Sg)	Fem. (Sg)	Neut. (Sg)	Masc. (Pl)	Fem. (Pl)	Neut. (Pl)
Nominative	quis	quis	quid	quī	quae	quae
Genitive	cúius	cúius	cúius	quórum	quárum	quórum
Dative	cui	cui	cui	quíbus	quíbus	quíbus
Accusative	quem	quem	quid	quōs	quās	quae
Ablative	quō	quō	quō	quíbus	quíbus	quíbus

VII. Regular Verbs

		1st Conjugation	2nd Conjugation	3rd Conjugation		4th Conjugation
	Infinitive	par**áre**	hab**ére**	mítt**ere**	iác**ere** (-iō)	aud**íre**
	Imperative	pár**ā**	háb**ē**	mítt**e**	iác**e**	aúd**ī**
		par**áte**	hab**éte**	mítt**ite**	iác**ite**	aud**íte**
Present	Singular 1	pár**ō**	hábe**ō**	mítt**ō**	iáci**ō**	aúdi**ō**
	2	pár**ās**	háb**ēs**	mítt**is**	iáci**s**	aúd**īs**
	3	pára**t**	hábe**t**	mítti**t**	iáci**t**	aúdi**t**
	Plural 1	par**ámus**	hab**émus**	mítti**mus**	iáci**mus**	aud**ímus**
	2	par**átis**	hab**étis**	mítti**tis**	iáci**tis**	aud**ítis**
	3	pára**nt**	hábe**nt**	mítt**unt**	iáciu**nt**	aúdiu**nt**
Imperfect	Singular 1	pará**bam**	habé**bam**	mittḗ**bam**	iacié**bam**	audié**bam**
	2	pará**bās**	habé**bās**	mittḗ**bās**	iacié**bās**	audié**bās**
	3	pará**bat**	habé**bat**	mittḗ**bat**	iacié**bat**	audié**bat**
	Plural 1	parābā́**mus**	habēbā́**mus**	mittēbā́**mus**	iaciēbā́**mus**	audiēbā́**mus**
	2	parābā́**tis**	habēbā́**tis**	mittēbā́**tis**	iaciēbā́**tis**	audiēbā́**tis**
	3	pará**bant**	habé**bant**	mittḗ**bant**	iacié**bant**	audié**bant**

VIII. Irregular Verbs

	Infinitive	ésse	pósse	vélle	nṓlle	férre	íre
	Imperative	es	—	—	nṓl**ī**	fer	ī
		és**te**	—	—	nōl**íte**	fér**te**	í**te**
Present	Singular 1	sum	pós**sum**	vól**ō**	nṓl**ō**	fér**ō**	é**ō**
	2	es	pót**es**	vī**s**	nōn vī**s**	fer**s**	ī**s**
	3	es**t**	pót**est**	vul**t**	nōn vul**t**	fer**t**	i**t**
	Plural 1	sú**mus**	pós**sumus**	vólu**mus**	nólu**mus**	féri**mus**	í**mus**
	2	és**tis**	pot**éstis**	vúl**tis**	nōn vúl**tis**	fér**tis**	í**tis**
	3	su**nt**	pós**sunt**	vólu**nt**	nólu**nt**	féru**nt**	éu**nt**
Imperfect	Singular 1	éra**m**	pót**eram**	volé**bam**	nōlé**bam**	feré**bam**	í**bam**
	2	érā**s**	pót**erās**	volé**bās**	nōlé**bās**	feré**bās**	í**bās**
	3	éra**t**	pót**erat**	volé**bat**	nōlé**bat**	feré**bat**	í**bat**
	Plural 1	erá**mus**	poterá**mus**	volēbā́**mus**	nōlēbā́**mus**	ferēbā́**mus**	ībā́**mus**
	2	erá**tis**	poterá**tis**	volēbā́**tis**	nōlēbā́**tis**	ferēbā́**tis**	ībā́**tis**
	3	éra**nt**	pót**erant**	volé**bant**	nōlé**bant**	feré**bant**	í**bant**

BUILDING THE MEANING

I. Parts of Speech

The following are eight basic parts of speech:

Nouns: names of persons, places, things, qualities, or acts (see page 4)

Pronouns: words that stand in place of nouns, e.g., *she* in place of *Cornelia*

Adjectives: words that describe persons, places, things, qualities, or acts (see page 4)

Verbs: words that denote actions (e.g., *sits*) or existence (e.g., *is*) (see page 4)

Adverbs: words that modify verbs, adjectives, or other adverbs (see pages 100–101)

Prepositions: words such as *from*, *in*, and *at*, which introduce prepositional phrases (see page 64)

Conjunctions: words that link other words, phrases, or clauses (see page 146)

Interjections: words that can stand alone and that call attention to a statement or express an emotion, e.g., *Look! Alas!*

II. Core Elements of Latin Sentences

You have met Latin sentences with the following combinations of core elements:

A. Subject and Intransitive Verb (see page 20)

> Cornēlia **sedet.** (1:3)   **Sedet** Cornēlia.   *Cornelia* **sits.**

This sentence has only a subject (S) and an intransitive verb (IV). **Cornēlia** is in the nominative case and is therefore the subject of the sentence.

The verb in the above sentence expresses an action that simply tells what the subject is doing. The action of the verb does not affect anyone or anything else. Verbs when so used are called intransitive verbs (IV).

B. Subject, Linking Verb, and Complement (see page 8)

> Cornēlia **est** puella.   *Cornelia* **is** *a girl.*
> Cornēlia puella **est.**

This sentence has a subject, **Cornēlia**, and a verb, **est**, as well as another word in the nominative case, **puella**. This word is linked to the subject by the verb **est**. The word **puella** is called a complement (C), because it completes the meaning of the sentence. **Est** is called a linking verb (LV) because it links the subject with the complement. The complement may appear before the linking verb, as in the second example above.

The linking verb in the following sentence links the subject with an adjective, which serves as a complement:

Cornēlia **est** laeta. (1:2–3)   *Cornelia **is** happy.*
Cornēlia laeta **est**.
Laeta **est** Cornēlia.
Laeta Cornēlia **est**.

C. Est/Sunt, Subject, No Complement (see page 8)

In pictūrā **est** puella. (1:1)   In pictūrā **sunt** puellae.
***There is** a girl in the picture.*   ***There are** girls in the picture.*

Note that **est** and **sunt** come before their subjects here.

D. Subject, Direct Object, and Transitive Verb (see page 20)

Sextus Cornēliam **vexat**. (4:1)   *Sextus **annoys** Cornelia.*

In this sentence there is a subject, a direct object (DO: see pages 20 and 40), and a verb. The direct object is in the accusative case, and it names the person or thing that receives the action of the verb. The verbs in such sentences are said to be transitive verbs (TV). The words in the Latin sentence could be arranged in any order and would express essentially the same meaning.

III. Sentence Types

Every Latin sentence expresses a statement, a command, an exclamation, or a question.

A. The following are statements:

In pictūrā est puella. (1:1)
There is a girl in the picture.

Flāvia scrībit. (1:5)
Flavia writes.

Sextus Cornēliam vexat. (4:1)
Sextus annoys Cornelia.

B. Sentences may express commands and have their verbs in the imperative (see page 74):

Dēscende, Sexte! (4:6)
Come down, Sextus!

Abīte, molestī! (3:8)
Go away, pests!

Negative commands are expressed with **nōlī** (singular) or **nōlīte** (plural) plus an infinitive (see page 74):

Nōlī servōs **excitāre**! (9:9)
Don't wake up the slaves!

C. A sentence may express an exclamation:

Quam celeriter appropinquat! (15:12)
How quickly it is approaching!

D. Statements can be turned into questions by placing an important word (often the verb) first and attaching the letters **-ne** to it (see page 13):

Puer ignāvus est.
The boy is cowardly.
(statement)

Est**ne** puer ignāvus? (5:4)
Is the boy cowardly?
(question)

Questions are often introduced by interrogative words such as the following:

Cuius...? *Whose...?* (sing.)
Cūr...? *Why...?*
Quālis...? *What sort of ...?*
Quandō...? *When...?*
Quem...? *Whom...?* (sing.)
Quī...? *Who...?* (pl.)
Quid...? *What...?*
Quis...? *Who...?* (sing.)
Quō...? *Where... to?*

Quōcum...? *With whom...?* (sing.)
Quō īnstrūmentō...? *With what instrument...? By what means...? How...?*
Quōmodo...? *In what manner...? How...?*
Quōs...? *Whom...?* (pl.)
Quot...? *How many...?*
Ubi...? *Where...?*
Unde...? *From where...?*

IV. More About Verbs

A. Tenses of Verbs

1. Verbs can be in the present tense, describing actions or situations in present time (see page 73):

   a. in a simple statement of fact:

   Cornelii Romam redīre **parant**.
   *The Cornelii **prepare** to return to Rome.*

b. in a description of an ongoing action:

Hodiē Cornēliī Rōmam redīre **parant**.
*Today the Cornelii **are preparing** to return to Rome.*

c. in a question:

Audītne Dāvus clāmōrem?
***Does** Davus **hear** the shouting?*

d. in an emphatic statement:

Clāmōrem ***audit***.
*He **does hear** the shouting.*

e. in a denial:

Clāmōrem nōn **audit**.
*He **does** not **hear** the shouting.*

2. The imperfect tense (see pages 98 and 106–107) shows action in the past that was:

a. going on for a time:

Ego et Mārcus **spectābāmus** cisium. (14:10)
*Marcus and I **were watching** the carriage.*

Cornēlia dormīre **volēbat**. (13:8)
*Cornelia **wanted** to sleep.*

b. repeated:

Mārcus **vexābat** Cornēliam. (13:7–8)
*Marcus **kept annoying** Cornelia.*

c. habitual or customary:

Dāvus in Britanniā **habitābat**.
*Davus **used to live** in Britain.*

d. beginning to happen:

Equōs ad raedam nostrum **dēvertēbat**. (14:11)
*He **began to turn** the horses **aside** in the direction of our carriage.*

B. Infinitives

The infinitive is the form of the verb marked by "to…" in English (e.g., "to walk") and by the letters *-re* in Latin (e.g., **err*āre*, rīd*ēre*, ascend*ere*,** and **dorm*īre***) (see page 26). You have seen three uses of the infinitive in Latin sentences:

1. The complementary infinitive (see page 26):

    Sextus arborēs **ascendere** <u>*vult*</u>.   *Sextus <u>wants</u> **to climb** trees.*

    Here the infinitive completes the meaning of the main verb. Other verbs and verbal phrases that are often completed with infinitives are: **nōlle, posse, parāre, solēre, timēre,** and **in animō habēre.**

2. The infinitive with impersonal verbal phrase (see page 34):

    <u>Necesse est</u> neque servum neque ancillam **reprehendere.** (6:14–15)
    *<u>It is necessary</u> **to scold** neither slave nor slave-woman.*

    Nōbīs <u>necesse est</u> statim **discēdere.** (9:13–14)
    *<u>It is necessary</u> for us **to leave** immediately.*

3. Accusative and infinitive with **docet** and **iubet** (see page 72):

    Aurēlia **Cornēliam** <u>docet</u> vīllam **cūrāre.** (6:11)
    *Aurelia <u>teaches</u> **Cornelia** (how) **to take care of** the country house.*

    Ancillam <u>iubet</u> aliās tunicās et stolās et pallās in cistam **pōnere.** (10:2)
    *<u>She orders</u> **the slave-woman to put** other tunics and stolas and pallas into a chest.*

V. Modifiers

There are many ways in which the thought expressed by a sentence can be elaborated and made fuller and clearer. For example, various kinds of modifiers can be used. Any noun or verb in a sentence can have modifiers.

A. Modifiers of Nouns

1. Adjectives may be used to modify nouns. They must agree with the nouns they modify in gender, case, and number (see pages 34–35 and 120–121):

    Flāvia in <u>vīllā</u> **vīcīnā** habitat. (1:4)
    *Flavia lives in a **neighboring** <u>country house</u>.*

    Cum <u>senātōre</u> **Rōmānō** iter facit. (page 121)
    *He travels with a **Roman** <u>senator</u>.*

2. Adjectives that modify the subject of the verb may sometimes best be translated as adverbs:

Brevī tempore, ubi Mārcus advenit, eum **laetae** excipiunt. (5:12–13)
*In a short time, when Marcus arrives, they welcome him **happily**.*

3. You have also seen a word or phrase in the genitive case used as a modifier (see page 80), usually with another noun. The genitive case relates or attaches one noun or phrase to another:

Dāvus ad portam **vīllae** stat. (11.17)
*Davus stands near the door **of the country house**.*

The genitive case sometimes indicates possession:

Vīlicus ipse vīllam **dominī** cūrat. (11:3)
*The overseer himself looks after **the master's** country house.*

You have also seen words or phrases in the genitive case used with adjectives, such as **plēnus** (see page 80):

Ārea est plēna **servōrum** et **ancillārum**. (11:4)
*The threshing floor is full **of slaves** and **slave-women**.*

4. For subordinate clauses that modify nouns, see section VIII: Main and Subordinate Clauses.

B. Modifiers of Verbs

1. Adverbs may be used to modify verbs (see page 100):

Laeta est Flāvia quod Cornēlia **iam** in vīllā habitat. (1:5)
*Flavia is happy because Cornelia is **now** living in the country house.*

Adverbs may express time (e.g., **adhūc**, *still*), place (e.g., **hīc**, *here*), or manner (e.g., **celeriter**, *quickly*) (see pages 100–101).

2. Nouns or phrases in the ablative case without a preposition may be used to modify verbs (see pages 90–91). Such nouns or phrases may indicate any of the following:

Cause:

Tuā culpā raeda est in fossā. (14:7)
***Because of your fault** the carriage is in the ditch.*
It's your fault that the carriage is in the ditch.

Instrument or Means:

Dāvus Getam **baculō** verberat. (12:17–18)
*Davus beats Geta **with his stick**.*

Dāvus Getam **tunicā** arripit. (12:17)
*Davus grabs hold of Geta **by the tunic**.*

Manner: a phrase consisting of a noun and adjective in the ablative case may be used to indicate *how* something happens. This is called the ablative of manner:

Tum venit Dāvus ipse et, "Tacēte, omnēs!" **magnā vōce** <u>clāmat</u>. (11:6)
*Then Davus himself comes, and <u>he shouts</u> **in a loud voice**, "Be quiet, everyone!"*

The preposition **cum** may be found in this construction when the noun is modified by an adjective, e.g., **magnā cum vōce**.

Respect:

In pictūrā est puella, **nōmine** Cornēlia. (1:1)
*There is a girl in the picture, Cornelia **with respect to her name/by name.***
*There is a girl in the picture, **named** Cornelia.*

Time When:

Etiam in pictūrā est vīlla rūstica ubi Cornēlia **aestāte** <u>habitat</u>. (1:2)
*Also in the picture there is a country house and farm where Cornelia <u>lives</u> **in the summer.***

Time within Which:

Brevī tempore Flāvia quoque <u>est</u> dēfessa. (2:4–5)
***In a short time** Flavia <u>is</u> also tired.*

3. Prepositional phrases usually modify verbs. Some prepositions are used with the accusative case (see page 64):

<u>ad</u> **vīllam** (2:7)	*to/toward **the country house***
Iānitor <u>ad</u> **iānuam** vīllae dormit. (9:3)	*The doorkeeper sleeps <u>near/at</u> **the door** of the country house.*
<u>in</u> **piscīnam** (3:8)	*<u>into</u> **the fishpond***
<u>per</u> **agrōs** (9:1)	*<u>through</u> **the fields***
<u>prope</u> **rīvum** (5:3)	*<u>near</u> **the stream***

With names of cities the accusative case is used without the preposition **ad** to express the idea "to":

"Eugepae!" clāmat Sextus, quī **Rōmam** īre vult. (7:14)
*"Hurray!" shouts Sextus, who wants to go **to Rome**.*

Some prepositions are used with the ablative case (see pages 64 and 90):

<u>ab</u> **urbe** (13:12)	*<u>from</u> **the city***
<u>cum</u> **canibus** (12:9)	*<u>with</u> **dogs***
<u>ē</u> **silvā**	*<u>out of</u> **the woods***

<u>ex</u> **agrīs** (2:7)	*out of* **the fields**
<u>in</u> **pictūrā** (1:1)	*in* **the picture**
<u>sub</u> **arbore** (1:3)	*under* **the tree**

4. For subordinate clauses that modify verbs, see section VIII: Main and Subordinate Clauses.

VI. Other Uses of Cases

A. The accusative case is used in exclamations:

    Ō mē miseram! (9:18)   ***Poor me**!*

B. The vocative case is used when addressing a person or persons directly (see page 56):

    Dēscende, **Sexte!** (4:7)   *Come down, **Sextus!***

VII. Conjunctions

Conjunctions (Latin **con-**, *together* + **iungere**, *to join*) are words that join things together. A conjunction may show a relationship between sentences. For example, **igitur**, *therefore*, indicates that a sentence describes the result or consequence of what was said in the previous sentence:

    Sextus est puer molestus quī semper Cornēliam vexat. Cornēlia **igitur** Sextum nōn amat. (4:1–2)
    *Sextus is an annoying boy who always annoys Cornelia. Cornelia, **therefore**, does not like Sextus.*

Other conjunctions may join elements within sentences that are added to one another and are of equal grammatical importance:

    Cornēlia <u>sedet</u> **et** <u>legit</u>. (1:3)
    *Cornelia <u>sits</u> **and** <u>reads</u>.*

    Etiam Sextus <u>dormit</u> **neque** Cornēliam <u>vexat</u>. (6:2)
    *Even Sextus <u>is sleeping</u> **and** <u>is</u> **not** <u>annoying</u> Cornelia.*

    Mārcus **neque** <u>ignāvus</u> **neque** <u>temerārius</u> est. (5:5–6)
    *Marcus is **neither** <u>cowardly</u> **nor** <u>rash</u>.*

    Hodiē puellae nōn <u>sedent</u> **sed** in agrīs <u>ambulant</u>. (2:2–3)
    *Today the girls <u>are</u> not <u>sitting</u> **but** <u>are walking</u> in the fields.*

VIII. Main and Subordinate Clauses

A clause is a group of words containing a verb. The following sentence contains two clauses, each of which is said to be a *main clause* because each could stand by itself as a complete sentence:

> Rīdent Mārcus et Cornēlia, sed nōn rīdet Sextus. (4:10–11)
> *Marcus and Cornelia laugh, but Sextus does not laugh.*

The clauses in this sentence are said to be *coordinate* (Latin **co-**, *together, same* + **ōrdō**, *order, rank*), and the conjunction that joins them, **sed**, is said to be a *coordinating conjunction*. For other coordinating conjunctions, see the examples in section VII: Conjunctions.

Subordinate (Latin **sub-**, *below* + **ōrdō**, *order, rank*) clauses are clauses that are of less grammatical importance than the main clause in a sentence. They are sometimes called dependent (Latin **dē-**, *down from* + **pendēre**, *to hang*) clauses because they hang down from the main clause and cannot stand by themselves. They are joined to the main clause by pronouns, adverbs, or conjunctions.

Subordinate clauses are modifiers. They may be descriptive, like adjectives, and modify nouns:

> Cornēlia est puella Rōmāna **quae** in Italiā habitat. (1:1–2)
> *Cornelia is a Roman girl **who** lives in Italy.*

> Etiam in pictūrā est vīlla rūstica **ubi** Cornēlia aestāte habitat. (1:2)
> *Also in the picture there is a country house and farm **where** Cornelia lives in the summer.*

But most subordinate clauses are adverbial, that is, they modify the verb of the main clause or the action of the main clause as a whole and are introduced by subordinating conjunctions that express ideas such as the following:

Cause:

> Cornēlia est laeta **quod** iam in vīllā habitat. (1:2–3)
> *Cornelia is happy **because** she now lives in the country house.*

Concession:

> **Quamquam** dominus abest, necesse est nōbīs strēnuē labōrāre. (11:7)
> ***Although** the master is away, it is necessary for us to work hard.*

Condition:

> **Sī** tū puer strēnuus es, ascende arborem!
> ***If** you are an energetic boy, climb a tree!*

Time:

> **Dum** Cornēlia legit, Flāvia scrībit. (1:4–5)
> *While Cornelia reads, Flavia writes.*

> **Dum** per viam ībant, Aurēlia et Cornēlia spectābant rūsticōs quī in agrīs labōrābant. (13:3–4)
> *While/As long as they were going along the road, Aurelia and Cornelia were looking at the peasants who were working in the fields.*

> Puerī, **ubi** clāmōrem audiunt, statim ad puellās currunt. (5:10)
> *The boys, **when** they hear the shout, immediately run to the girls.*

PRONUNCIATION OF LATIN

Consonants

The Latin alphabet does not have the letters *j* or *w*; the letter *i* before a vowel is a consonant and is pronounced as *y*, and *v* is pronounced as *w*. The letters *k*, *y*, and *z* occur in few Latin words, the latter two letters only in words taken over by the Romans from their neighbors the Greeks.

In pronouncing Latin you will find the following rules of use.

Most consonants are pronounced as in English, but the following should be noted:
b before **s** or **t** is pronounced as English *p*: **urbs, observat.**
c is always hard and pronounced as English *k*: **cadit.**
g is hard, as in English "get": **gemit.**
gn in the middle of a word may be pronounced as the *ngn* in English "hangnail":
   magnus.
i before a vowel is a consonant and is pronounced as English *y*: **iam.**
r should be rolled: **rāmus.**
s is pronounced as in English "sing," never as in "roses": **servus.**
v is pronounced as English *w*: **vīlla.**

Vowels

The following approximations are offered for the pronounciation of short and long vowels. In addition, long vowels should be held approximately twice as long as short vowels.

Short	Long
a – English "aha" (**ad**)	**ā** = English "father" (**clāmat**)
e = English "pet" (**ex**)	**ē** = English "date" (**dēscendit**)
i = English "sip" (**Italia**)	**ī** = English "sleep" (**īrātus**)
o = English "for" (**arborem**)	**ō** = English "holy" (**in hortō**)
u = English "foot" (**ubi**)	**ū** = English "boot" (**fūrtim**)

The diphthong **ae** is pronounced as the *y* in English "sky" (**amīcae**). The diphthong **au** is pronounced as the *ow* in English "how" (**audit**). The diphthong **ei** is pronounced as the "ay" in English "say" (**deinde**).

Syllables

In dividing Latin words into syllables, note the following rules:

1. A single consonant between two vowels usually goes with the second vowel:

    nō-mi-ne   Rō-mā-na   vī-cī-na

2. Two consonants between vowels are usually divided between the syllables:

    pu-el-la   pic-tū-ra   rūs-ti-ca

Accents

Latin words are accented according to simple rules:

1. If the next to the last syllable (the *penult*) has a long vowel or a diphthong, it will receive the accent:

    discédō

2. If the penult has a short vowel followed by two consonants, it will usually receive the accent:

    exténdō

3. Otherwise, the accent falls on the third syllable from the end (the *antepenult*):

    Británnicus

4. Almost all words of two syllables are accented on the first syllable:

    For example: **légit**   Exception: **adhŭ́c**

Careful observation of the long marks (macrons) over vowels will thus help with both pronunciation and accenting of Latin words.

LATIN TO ENGLISH VOCABULARY

Latin words in boldface are for mastery; those not in boldface are for recognition (see Introduction, page xv). Numbers in parentheses at the end of entries refer to the chapters in which the words appear in vocabulary entries or in Building the Meaning or Forms sections. Roman numerals refer to Review chapters.

A

ā or **ab**, prep. + abl., *from* (13)
ábeō, abíre, irreg., *to go away* (3, 9)
  Ábī!/Abíte! *Go away!* (3)
ábsum, abésse, irreg., *to be away, be absent, be distant* (11)
áccidit, accídere, *(it) happens* (14)
ad, prep. + acc., *to, toward, at, near* (2, 9)
adhúc, adv., *still* (5, 13)
ádiuvō, adiuvāre, *to help* (6)
advéniō, advenīre, *to reach, arrive (at)* (5)
advesperáscit, advesperáscere, *it gets dark* (17)
aedifícium, -ī, n., *building* (17)
aéstās, aestátis, f., *summer* (1)
  aestáte, *in the summer* (1, 12)
áger, ágrī, m., *field* (2)
ágō, ágere, *to do, drive* (8, 14)
  Áge!/Ágite! *Come on!* (8)
álius, ália, áliud, *another, other* (10)
  áliī...áliī..., *some...others...* (9)
  álius...álius, *one...another*
álter, áltera, álterum, *second, one (of two), the other (of two), another* (1)
  álter...álter, *the one...the other* (16)
ámbulō, ambuláre, *to walk* (2)
amíca, -ac, f., *friend* (2)
amícus, -ī, m., *friend* (3)
ámō, amáre, *to like, love* (4)
ancílla, -ae, f., *slave-woman* (6)
ánimus, -ī, m., *mind* (16)
  in ánimō habére, *to intend* (16)

apériō, aperíre, *to open* (16)
appáreō, appārére, *to appear* (15)
appropínquō, appropinquáre + **ad** + acc., *to approach, to come near (to)* (4)
ápud, prep. + acc., *at the house of, with, in front of, before* (16)
áqua, -ae, f., *water* (6)
árbor, árboris, f., *tree* (1)
área, -ae, f., *open space, threshing floor* (11)
arrípiō, arrípere, *to grab hold of, snatch, seize* (5)
ars, ártis, gen. pl., **ártium**, f., *skill* (14)
ascéndō, ascéndere, *to climb, climb into (a carriage)* (4)
aúdiō, audíre, *to hear, listen to* (4)
auríga, -ae, m., *charioteer* (13)
auxílium, -ī, n., *help* (5, 15)
  Fer/Férte auxílium! *Bring help! Help!* (5)

B

báculum, -ī, n., *stick, staff* (10, 15)
Báiae, -árum, f. pl., *Baiae*
bónus, -a, -um, *good* (12)
bōs, bóvis, m./f., *ox, cow* (15)
brévī témpore, *in a short time, soon* (2, 12)
Británnia, -ae, f., *Britain* (8)
Británnicus, -a, -um, *British* (3)

C

cádō, cádere, *to fall* (3)
caélum, -ī, n., *sky* (17)
cálidus, -a, -um, *warm* (5)
cánis, cánis, m./f., *dog* (12)
cāríssimus, -a, -um, *dearest* (16)
caúpō, caupónis, m., *innkeeper* (17)
caupóna, -ae, f., *inn* (17)
cáveō, cavére, *to be careful, watch out (for), beware (of)* (4, 13)

Cávē!/Cavéte! *Be careful! Watch out (for)! Beware (of)!* (4, 13)

celériter, adv., *quickly* (8, 13)

celérrimē, adv., *very fast, very quickly* (14)

célō, cēláre, *to hide* (11)

céntum, *a hundred* (15)

céssō, cessáre, *to be idle, do nothing, delay* (14)

cíbus, -ī, m., *food* (6)

císium, -ī, n., *light two-wheeled carriage* (14, 15)

císta, -ae, f., *trunk, chest* (10)

cívis, cívis, gen. pl., **cívium,** m./f., *citizen* (13)

clámō, clāmáre, *to shout* (3)

clámor, clāmóris, m., *shout, shouting* (5)

commótus, -a, -um, *moved* (14)

compléxū, *in an embrace* (9)

cóncidō, concídere, *to fall down* (14)

cōnspíciō, cōnspícere, *to catch sight of* (4)

cónsulō, cōnsúlere, *to consult* (7)

cónvocō, convocáre, *to call together* (12)

cóquō, cóquere, *to cook* (6)

Cornēliánus, -a, um, *belonging to Cornelius, Cornelian* (10)

crās, adv., *tomorrow* (10, 13)

cubículum, -ī, n., *room, bedroom* (8, 15)

cúlpa, -ae, f., *fault, blame* (14)

cum, prep. + abl., *with* (12)

cúnctī, -ae, -a, *all* (14)

Cūr…? adv., *Why…?* (1)

cúrō, cūráre, *to look after, take care of* (6)

cúrrō, cúrrere, *to run* (2)

custódiō, custōdíre, *to guard* (17)

D

dē, prep. + abl., *down from, concerning, about* (16)

décem, *ten* (15)

dēféndō, dēféndere, *to defend* (I)

dēféssus, -a, -um, *tired* (2)

deínde, adv., *then, next* (8, 13)

dēscéndō, dēscéndere, *to come/go down, climb down* (4)

dēvértō, dēvértere, *to turn aside* (14)

díēs, diéī, m., *day* (5, 13)

discédō, discédere, *to go away, depart* (9)

díū, adv., *for a long time* (15)

dóceō, docére, *to teach* (6)

dómina, -ae, f., *mistress, lady of the house* (17)

dóminus, -ī, m., *master, owner* (11)

dórmiō, dormíre, *to sleep* (4)

dúcō, dúcere, *to lead, take, bring* (7)

dum, conj., *while, as long as* (1)

dúo, dúae, dúo, *two* (15)

E

ē or **ex,** prep. + abl., *from, out of* (2, 5, 9)

eádem, *the same* (3)

éam, *her, it* (9, 16)

Écce! interj., *Look! Look at!* (1)

effúgiō, effúgere, *to flee, run away, escape* (11)

égo, *I* (5)

Ēheu! interj., *Alas! Oh no!* (7)

éius, *his, her(s), its* (2)

éō, íre, irreg., *to go* (7, 17)

éō ípsō témpore, *at that very moment* (10)

éōs, *them* (5)

epístula, -ae, f., *letter* (7)

équus, -ī, m., *horse* (10)

érat, *(he/she/it) was* (13)

érrō, erráre, *to wander* (5)

ésse (see **sum**)

est, *(he/she/it) is* (1)

et, conj., *and* (1)

étiam, adv., *also, even* (1, 6, 13)

Eúgepae! interj., *Hurray!* (7)

éum, *him, it* (5)

ex or **ē,** prep. + abl., *from, out of* (2, 5, 9)

excípiō, excípere, *to welcome, receive, catch* (5, 16)

excítō, excitáre, *to rouse, wake (someone) up* (8)

exclámō, exclāmáre, *to exclaim, shout out* (10)

éxeō, exíre, irreg., *to go out* (5)

exspéctō, exspectáre, *to look out for, wait for* (15)

éxtrahō, extráhere, *to drag out, take out* (14)

F

fáciō, fácere, *to make, do* (1)

íter fácere, *to travel* (13)

Quid fácit…? *What does…do? What is… doing?* (1)

fátuus, -a, -um, *stupid* (13)

fémina, -ae, f., *woman* (3)
fériō, feríre, *to hit, strike* (16)
férō, férre, irreg., *to bring, carry* (5, 12, 17)
   Fer/Férte auxílium! *Bring help! Help!* (5)
feróciter, adv., *fiercely* (13)
festínō, festīnáre, *to hurry* (9)
fília, -ae, f., *daughter* (11)
fílius, -ī, m., *son* (11)
fortásse, adv., *perhaps* (15)
fóssa, -ae, f., *ditch* (12)
frágor, fragóris, m., *crash, noise, din* (4)
fráter, frátris, m., *brother* (11)
frígidus, -a, -um, *cool, cold* (5)
frōns, fróntis, gen. pl., fróntium, f., *forehead* (12)
frústrā, adv., *in vain* (14)
fúrtim, adv., *stealthily* (4, 13)

G

gaúdeō, gaudére, *to be glad, rejoice* (14)
gémō, gémere, *to groan* (3)
gérō, gérere, *to wear* (10)
Graécus, -a, -um, *Greek* (17)
   Graécī, -órum, m. pl., *the Greeks* (I)

H

hábeō, habére, *to have, hold* (10)
   in ánimō habére, *to intend* (16)
hábitō, habitáre, *to live, dwell* (1)
haéreō, haerére, *to stick* (14)
hīc, adv., *here* (9, 13)
hódiē, adv., *today* (2, 13)
hóminēs, hóminum, m. pl., *people* (15)
hóra, -ae, f., *hour* (9)
hórtus, -ī, m., *garden* (3)
hóspes, hóspitis, m./f., *host, guest, friend* (16)

I

iáciō, iácere, *to throw* (10)
iam, adv., *now, already* (1, 8, 13)
   nōn iam, adv., *no longer* (2, 13)
iánitor, iānitóris, m., *doorkeeper* (9)
iánua, -ae, f., *door* (9)
íbi, adv., *there* (5, 13)

id quod, *that which, what* (11)
ídem, éadem, ídem, *the same* (3)
idéntidem, adv., *again and again, repeatedly* (13)
ígitur, conj., *therefore* (4)
ignávus, -a, -um, *cowardly, lazy* (5)
ílle, ílla, íllud, *that, he, she, it,* (11, 15, 16)
   illā nocte, *that night* (11)
immóbilis, -is, -e, *motionless* (12)
impédiō, impedíre, *to hinder, prevent* (11)
in, prep. + abl., *in, on* (1, 9)
   in ánimō habére, *to intend* (16)
   in itínere, *on a journey* (10)
in, prep. + acc., *into, against* (3, 9)
íncitō, incitáre, *to spur on, urge on, drive* (10)
incólumis, -is, -e, *unhurt, safe and sound* (14)
índuō, indúere, *to put on* (8)
īnfírmus, -a, -um, *weak, shaky* (4)
ínquit, *(he/she) says, said* (7)
intéreā, adv., *meanwhile* (10, 13)
interpéllō, interpelláre, *to interrupt* (14)
íntrō, intráre, *to enter, go into* (8)
inúrō, inúrere, *to brand* (12)
invéniō, inveníre, *to come upon, find* (12)
iócus, -ī, m., *joke, prank* (16)
   per iócum, *as a prank* (16)
ípse, ípsa, ípsum, *himself, herself, itself,*
   themselves, very (6, 10)
íra, -ae, f., *anger* (11)
īrátus, -a, -um, *angry* (3)
íre (see **éō**) (7, 17)
íta, adv., *thus, so, in this way* (3, 13)
Íta vérō! adv., *Yes! Indeed!* (3, 13)
Itália, -ae, f., *Italy* (1)
ítaque, adv., *and so, therefore* (16)
íter, itíneris, n., *journey* (10, 13, 15)
   íter fácere, *to travel* (13)
íterum, adv., *again, a second time* (8, 13)
iúbeō, iubére, *to order, bid* (10)

L

labórō, laboráre, *to work* (3)
   labōrántēs, *working* (7)
lácrimō, lacrimáre, *to weep, cry* (9)
   lácrimāns, *weeping* (9)
laétus, -a, -um, *happy, glad* (1)

lána, -ae, f., *wool* (6)
    lánam tráhere, *to spin wool* (6)
látrō, lātráre, *to bark* (12)
légō, légere, *to read* (1)
léntē, adv., *slowly* (2, 13)
líberī, -órum, m. pl., *children* (10, 11)
líttera, -ae, f., *letter (of the alphabet)* (12)
lóngus, -a, -um, *long* (15)
lúcet, lūcére, lúxit, *it is light, it is day* (6)
lúdō, lúdere, *to play* (16)
    pílā lúdere, *to play ball* (16)
lúpa, -ae, f., *she-wolf* (II)
lúpus, -ī, m., *wolf* (5)

M

mágnus, -a, -um, *big, great, large, loud (voice, laugh)* (4)
    mágnā vóce, *in a loud voice* (4)
    mágnō rīsū, *with a loud laugh* (13)
máneō, manére, *to remain, stay, wait (for)* (9)
máter, mátris, f., *mother* (6, 11)
mē, *me* (4)
    mécum, *with me* (9)
méus, -a, -um, *my, mine* (7)
míhi, *for me, to me* (8)
mílle, *a thousand* (15)
Mínimē! *No! Not at all!* (3, 13)
míser, mísera, míserum, *unhappy, miserable, wretched* (9)
míttō, míttere, *to send* (9)
moléstus, -a, -um, *troublesome, annoying* (4)
    moléstus, -ī, m., *pest* (3)
mórtuus, -a, -um, *dead* (16)
móveō, movére, *to move* (14)
mox, adv., *soon, presently* (6, 13)
múltī, -ae, -a, *many* (3)
múrmur, múrmuris, n., *murmur, rumble* (15)
mússō, mussáre, *to mutter* (11)

N

nam, conj., *for* (8)
nārrátor, nārrātóris, m., *narrator* (8)
-ne (indicates a yes or no question) (3)
Neápolis, Neápolis, f., *Naples* (15)
necésse, adv. or indeclinable adj., *necessary* (6)

némō, néminis, m./f., *no one* (9)
néque, conj., *and...not* (6)
    néque...néque, conj., *neither...nor* (5)
nésciō, nescíre, *to be ignorant, not to know* (9)
níhil, *nothing* (4)
nóbīs, *for us* (9)
    nōbíscum, *with us* (16)
nócte, *at night* (12)
nólō, nólle, irreg., *not to wish, not to want, to be unwilling* (5, 17)
    Nólī/Nólīte + infin., *Don't...!* (9)
nómen, nóminis, n., *name* (1, 15)
    nómine, *by name, named* (1)
nōn, adv., *not* (2, 13)
    nōn iam, adv., *no longer* (2, 13)
nóndum, adv., *not yet* (6, 13)
nónus, -a, -um, *ninth* (16)
nōs, *we, us* (8)
nóster, nóstra, nóstrum, *our* (14)
nóvem, *nine* (15)
nóvus, -a, -um, *new* (16)
nox, nóctis, gen. pl., **nóctium,** f., *night* (11)
    íllā nócte, *that night* (11)
    nócte, *at night* (12)
núbēs, núbis, gen. pl., **núbium,** f., *cloud* (15)
núllus, -a, -um, *no, not any* (9)
númerus, -ī, m., *number* (11)
nunc, adv., *now* (6, 13)
núntius, -ī, m., *messenger* (7)

O

ō, interj., used with vocative and in exclamations (9)
    Ō mē míseram! *Poor me! Oh dear me!* (9)
obsérvō, obserráe, *to watch* (6)
occupátus, -a, -um, *busy* (7)
óctō, *eight* (15)
olfáciō, olfácere, *to catch the scent of, smell, sniff* (12)
olīvétum, -ī, n., *olive grove* (14, 15)
ómnēs, *all, everyone* (6)
    ómnia quae, *everything that* (6)
ónus, óneris, n., *load, burden* (15)

P

pálla, -ae, f., *palla* (10)
parátus, -a, -um, *ready, prepared* (10)

párēns, paréntis, m./f., *parent* (11)
párō, paráre, *to prepare, get ready* (5, 20)
pars, pártis, gen. pl., **pártium,** f., *part, direction, region* (13)
páter, pátris, m., *father* (6, 11)
per, prep. + acc., *through, along* (6, 9)
   per iócum, *as a prank* (16)
perīculósus, -a, -um, *dangerous* (17)
perículum, -ī, n., *danger* (14, 15)
pernóctō, pernoctáre, *to spend the night* (17)
pertérritus, -a, -um, *frightened, terrified* (5)
pēs, pédis, m., *foot* (13)
pétō, pétere, *to look for, seek, head for, aim at, attack* (5)
pictúra, -ae, f., *picture* (1)
píla, -ae, f., *ball* (16)
   pílā lúdere, *to play ball* (16)
piscína, -ae, f., *fishpond* (3)
plácidē, adv., *gently, peacefully* (14)
plaústrum, -ī, n., *wagon, cart* (15)
plḗnus, -a, -um, *full* (11)
Pompéiī, -órum, m. pl., *Pompeii*
pónō, pónere, *to put, place* (10)
pórta, -ae, f., *gate* (11)
pórtō, portáre, *to carry* (6)
póssum, pósse, irreg., *to be able; I can* (5, 14)
   póterat, *(he/she/it) was able, could* (13)
   pótest, *(he/she/it) is able, can* (5)
praeclárus, -a, -um, *distinguished, famous* (13)
praetéreā, adv., *besides, too, moreover* (15)
praetéreō, praeteríre, irreg., *to go past* (15)
praetéxta, tóga, -ae, f., *toga with purple border* (10)
prínceps, príncipis, m., *emperor* (7)
prócul, adv., *in the distance, far off, far* (15)
prōmíttō, prōmíttere, *to promise* (9)
própe, prep. + acc., *near* (5, 9)
puélla, -ae, f., *girl* (1)
púer, púerī, m., *boy* (3)
púlvis, púlveris, m., *dust* (15)
púrgō, pūrgáre, *to clean* (6)

Q

quae, *who* (1, 11)
Quális…? Quális…? Quále…? *What sort of…?* (4)
Quam…! adv., *How…!* (13)
quámquam, conj., *although* (11)

Quándō…? adv., *When…?* (12)
quáttuor, *four* (15)
Quem…? *Whom…?* (5)
quī, quae, quod, *who, which, that* (1, 3, 14)
Quī…? *Who…?* (pl.) (6)
Quibúscum…? *With whom…?* (12)
Quid…? *What…?* (1, 4)
   Quid fácit…? *What does…do? What is…doing?* (1)
quídam, quaédam, quóddam, *a certain* (10)
quiésco, quiéscere, *to rest, keep quiet* (13)
quīngéntī, -ae, -a, *five hundred* (15)
quīnquāgíntā, *fifty* (15)
quínque, *five* (15)
Quis…? Quid…? *Who…? What…?* (1, 4)
   Quid facit…? *What does…do? What is…doing?* (1)
Quō…? adv., *Where…to?* (4)
Quócum…? *With whom…?* (12)
quod, conj., *because* (1)
quod, *which, that* (14)
Quō īnstrūméntō…? *With what instrument…? By what means…? How?* (12)
Quómodo…? adv., *In what manner…? In what way…? How…?* (12)
quóque, adv., *also* (2, 13)
Quōs…? *Whom…?* (7)
Quot…? *How many…?* (15)

R

raéda, -ae, f., *carriage* (10)
raedárius, -ī, m., *coachman, driver* (10)
rámus, -ī, m., *branch* (4)
rédeō, redíre, irreg., *to return, go back* (7)
relínquō, relínquere, *to leave behind* (16)
repéllō, repéllere, *to drive off, drive back* (5)
reprehéndō, reprehéndere, *to blame, scold, reprove* (6)
respóndeō, respondére, *to reply* (5)
révocō, revocáre, *to recall, call back* (7)
rídeō, rīdére, *to laugh (at), smile* (3)
rísū, mágnō, *with a loud laugh* (13)
rívus, -ī, m., *stream* (5)
rógō, rogáre, *to ask* (12)
Róma, -ae, f., *Rome* (7)
   Rómam, *to Rome* (7)

Rōmánus, -a, -um, *Roman* (1)

    Rōmánī, -órum, m. pl., *the Romans* (III)

róta, -ae, f., *wheel* (15)

rústica, vílla, -ae, f., *country house and farm* (1)

rústicus, -ī, m., *peasant* (13)

S

saépe, adv., *often* (2, 13)

salútō, salūtáre, *to greet, welcome* (7)

Sálvē!/Salvéte! *Greetings! Hello!* (7)

sálvus, -a, -um, *safe* (5)

sceléstus, -a, -um, *wicked* (10)

scíō, scíre, *to know* (16)

scríbō, scríbere, *to write* (1)

sē, *himself, herself, oneself, itself, themselves* (11)

secúndus, -a, -um, *second* (9)

sed, conj., *but* (2)

sédeō, sedére, *to sit* (1)

sēmisómnus, -a, -um, *half-asleep* (9)

sémper, adv., *always* (4, 13)

senátor, senātóris, m., *senator* (7)

sénex, sénis, m., *old man* (I)

séptem, *seven* (15)

séptimus, -a, -um, *seventh* (13)

sérvus, -ī, m., *slave* (3)

sex, *six* (15)

sī, conj., *if* (5)

siléntium, -ī, n., *silence* (15)

sílva, -ae, f., *woods, forest* (5)

símul, adv., *together, at the same time* (9, 13)

sóleō, solére + infin., *to be accustomed (to), be in the habit (of)* (10)

sollícitus, -a, -um, *anxious, worried* (4)

sólus, -a, -um, *alone* (3)

sóror, soróris, f., *sister* (11)

spéctō, spectáre, *to watch, look at* (7)

státim, adv., *immediately* (5, 13)

státua, -ae, f., *statue* (3)

stō, stáre, *to stand* (10)

stóla, -ae, f., *stola (a woman's outer garment)* (10)

strénuus, -a, -um, *active, energetic* (2)

    strénuē, adv., *strenuously, hard* (6, 13)

sub, prep. + abl., *under, beneath* (1, 9)

súbitō, adv., *suddenly* (3, 13)

sum, ésse, irreg., *to be* (1, 14)

sunt, *(they) are* (2)

súrgō, súrgere, *to get up, rise* (6)

súus, -a, -um, *his, her, its, their (own)* (9)

T

tabellárius, -ī, m., *courier* (13)

táceō, tacére, *to be quiet* (9)

    Tácē!/Tacéte! *Be quiet!* (9)

tácitē, adv., *silently* (9, 13)

taédet, taedére, *it bores* (16)

támen, adv., *however, nevertheless* (6, 13)

tándem, adv., *at last, at length* (2, 13)

tántum, adv., *only* (15)

tárdus, -a, -um, *slow* (15)

tē (see **tū**), *you* (4)

temerárius, -a, -um, *rash, reckless, bold* (5)

témptō, temptáre, *to try* (9)

témpus, témporis, n., *time* (2, 8, 12, 15)

    brévī témpore, *in a short time, soon* (2, 12)

    éō ípsō témpore, *at that very moment* (10)

téneō, tenére, *to hold* (9)

térreō, terrére, *to frighten, terrify* (4)

tímeō, timére, *to fear, be afraid (to/of)* (5)

tóga, -ae, f., *toga* (8)

    tóga praetéxta, *toga with purple border* (10)

trádō, trádere, *to hand over* (7)

tráhō, tráhere, *to drag, pull* (6, 12)

    lánam tráhere, *to spin wool* (6)

trēs, trēs, tría, *three* (13, 15)

    tríbus diébus, *in three days* (12, 13)

Tróia, -ae, f., *Troy* (I)

Troiánus, -a, -um, *Trojan* (I)

    Troiánī, -órum, m. pl., *the Trojans* (I)

tū (acc. **tē**), *you* (sing.) (4)

tum, adv., *at that moment, then* (4, 13)

túnica, -ae, f., *tunic* (8)

túus, -a, -um, *your* (sing.) (9)

U

úbi, conj., *where* (1), *when* (5)

Úbi...? adv., *Where...?* (10, 12)

Únde...? adv., *From where...?* (12)

ūndécimus, -a, -um, *eleventh* (17)

únus, -a, -um, *one* (15)
urbs, úrbis, gen. pl., **úrbium,** f., *city* (7)
ut, conj., *as* (16)
úxor, uxóris, f., *wife* (11)

V

Válē!/Valéte! *Goodbye!* (9)
vehículum, -ī, n., *vehicle* (13, 15)
vélle (see **vólō**)
véniō, veníre, *to come* (7)
vérberō, vērleráre, *to beat, whip* (11)
vértō, vértere, *to turn* (16)
vēstígium, -ī, n., *track, footprint, trace* (12, 15)
véxō, vexáre, *to annoy* (4)
vía, -ae, f., *road, street* (10)
   Vía Áppia, -ae, f., *the Appian Way* (11)
vīcínus, -a, -um, *neighboring, adjacent* (1)

vídeō, vidére, *to see* (4)
vílicus, -ī, m., *overseer, farm manager* (11)
vílla, -ae, f., *country house* (1)
   vílla rústica, -ae, f., *country house and farm* (1)
vínea, -ae, f., *vineyard* (12)
vir, vírī, m., *man, husband* (3, 11)
vírga, -ae, f., *stick, rod, switch* (13)
vīs (from **vólō**), *you want* (16)
vítō, vītáre, *to avoid* (13)
vócō, -áre, *to call* (16)
vólō, vélle, irreg., *to wish, want, be willing* (5, 17)
vōs, *you* (pl.) (8)
vōx, vócis, f., *voice* (4)
   mágnā vóce, *in a loud voice* (4)
vult (from **vólō**), *(he/she) wishes, wants, is willing* (5, 17)

ENGLISH TO LATIN VOCABULARY

All Latin words in this list are in boldface, regardless of whether they are for mastery or for recognition (see Introduction, page xv). Numbers in parentheses at the end of entries refer to the chapters in which the words appear in vocabulary entries or in Building the Meaning or Forms sections. Roman numerals refer to Review sections.

A

able, (he/she/it) was, **póterat** (13)
able, to be, **póssum, pósse** (5, 14)
about, **dē,** prep. + abl. (16)
absent, to be, **ábsum, abésse** (11)
accustomed (to), to be, **sóleō, solére** + inf. (10)
active, **strénuus, -a, -um** (2)
adjacent, **vīcínus, -a, -um (1)**
afraid (to/of), to be, **tímeō, timére** (5)
again, **íterum,** adv. (8, 13)
again and again, **idéntidem,** adv. (13)
against, **in,** prep. + acc. (3, 9)
aim at, to, **pétō, pétere** (5)
Alas! **Éheu!** interj. (7)
all, **cúnctī, -ae, -a** (14), **ómnis, -is, -e** (6)
alone, **sólus, -a, -um** (3)
along, **per,** prep. + acc. (6, 9)
already, **iam,** adv. (1, 8, 13)
also, **étiam,** adv. (1, 6, 13), **quóque,** adv. (2, 13)
although, **quámquam,** conj. (11)
always, **sémper,** adv. (4, 13)
and, **et,** conj. (1)
and...not, **néque,** conj. (6)
and so, **ítaque,** adv. (16)
anger, **íra, -ae,** f. (11)
angry, **īrátus, -a, -um** (3)
annoy, to, **véxō, vexáre** (4)
annoying, **moléstus, -a, -um** (4)
another, **álius, ália, áliud** (10)

álter, áltera, álterum (1)
anxious, **sollícitus, -a, -um** (4)
appear, to, **appáreō, appārére** (15)
Appian Way, the, **Vía Áppia, -ae,** f. (11)
approach, to, **appropínquō, appropinquáre** + **ad** + acc. (4)
are, they, **sunt** (2)
arrive (at), to, **advéniō, adveníre** (5)
as, **ut,** conj. (16)
as a prank, **per iócum** (16)
as long as, **dum,** conj. (1)
ask, to, **rógō, rogáre** (12)
at, **ad,** prep. + acc. (2, 9)
at last, **tándem,** adv. (2, 13)
at length, **tándem,** adv. (2, 13)
at night, **nócte** (12)
at the house of, **ápud,** prep. + acc. (16)
attack, to, **pétō, pétere** (5)
attend to, to, **cúrō, cūráre** (6)
avoid, to, **vítō, vītáre** (13)
away, to be, **ábsum, abésse** (11)

B

Baiae, **Báiae, -árum,** f. pl.
ball, **píla, -ae,** f. (16)
ball, to play, **pílā lúdere** (16)
bark, to, **látrō, lātráre** (12)
barking, **lātrāns** (18)
be, to, **sum, ésse** (1, 14)
be away, to, **ábsum, abésse** (11)
Be careful! **Cávē!/Cavéte!** (4, 13)
be careful, to, **cáveō, cavére** (4, 13)
Be quiet! **Tácē!/Tacéte!** (9)
bear, to, **férō, férre** (16)
beat, to, **vérberō, verberáre** (11)
because, **quod,** conj. (1, 13)
bedroom, **cubículum, -ī,** n. (8, 15)
beneath, **sub,** prep. + abl. (1, 9)
besides, **praetéreā,** adv. (15)

Beware (of)! **Cávē!/Cavéte!** (4, 13)
beware (of), to, **cáveō, cavére** (4, 13)
bid, to, **iúbeō, iubére** (10)
big, **mágnus, -a, -um** (4)
blame, **cúlpa, -ae,** f. (14)
blame, to, **reprehéndō, reprehéndere** (6)
bold, **temerárius, -a, -um** (5)
bores, it, **taédet, taedére** (16)
boy, **púer, púerī,** m. (3)
branch, **rámus, -ī,** m. (4)
brand, to, **inúrō, inúrere** (12)
bring, to, **dúcō, dúcere** (7)
Bring help! **Fer/Férte auxílium!** (5)
Britain, **Británnia, -ae,** f. (8)
British, **Británnicus, -a, -um** (3)
brother, **fráter, frátris,** m. (11)
building, **aedifícium, -ī,** n. (17)
burden, **ónus, óneris,** n. (15)
busy, **occupátus, -a, -um** (7)
but, **sed,** conj. (2)
By what means...? **Quō īnstrūméntō...?** (12)

C

call, to, **vócō, vocáre** (16)
call back, to, **révocō, revocáre** (7)
call together, to, **cónvocō, convocáre** (12)
can, I, **póssum, pósse** (5, 14)
can, he/she/it, **pótest** (5)
careful! Be, **Cávē!/Cavéte!** (4, 13)
careful, to be, **cáveō, cavére** (4, 13)
carriage, **raéda, -ae,** f. (10)
carriage, light two-wheeled, **císium, -ī,** n. (14, 15)
carry, to, **férō, férre** (5, 12), **pórtō, portáre** (6)
cart, **plaústrum, -ī,** n. (15)
catch, to, **excípiō, excípere** (5, 16)
catch sight of, to, **cōnspíciō, cōnspícere** (4)
catch the scent of, to, **olfáciō, olfácere** (12)
certain, (a), **quídam, quaédam, quóddam** (10)
charioteer, **auríga, -ae,** m. (13)
chest, **císta, -ae,** f. (10)
children, **líberī, -órum,** m. pl. (10, 11)
citizen, **cívis, cívis,** gen. pl., **cívium,** m./f. (13)
city, **urbs, úrbis,** gen. pl., **úrbium,** f. (7)

clean, to, **púrgō, pūrgáre** (6)
climb, to, **ascéndō, ascéndere** (4)
climb down, to, **dēscéndō, dēscéndere** (4)
climb into (a carriage), to, **ascéndō, ascéndere** (4)
cloud, **núbēs, núbis,** gen. pl., **núbium,** f. (15)
coachman, **raedárius, -ī,** m. (10)
cold, **frígidus, -a, -um** (5)
come, to, **véniō, veníre** (7)
come down, to, **dēscéndō, dēscéndere** (4)
come near (to), to, **appropínquō, appropinquáre** + **ad** + acc. (4)
Come on! **Áge!/Ágite!** (8)
come upon, to, **invéniō, inveníre** (12)
concerning, **dē,** prep. + abl. (16)
consult, to, **cónsulō, cōnsúlere** (7)
cook, to, **cóquō, cóquere** (6)
cool, **frígidus, -a, -um** (5)
Cornelian, **Cornēliánus, -a, -um** (10)
Cornelius, belonging to, **Cornēliánus, -a, -um** (10)
could, (he/she/it), **póterat** (13)
country house, **vílla, -ae,** f. (1)
country house and farm, **vílla rústica, -ae,** f. (1)
courier, **tabellárius, -ī,** m. (13)
cow, **bōs, bóvis,** m./f. (15)
cowardly, **ignávus, -a, -um** (5)
crash, **frágor, fragóris,** m. (4)
cry, to, **lácrimō, lacrimáre** (9)

D

danger, **perículum, -ī,** n. (14, 15)
dangerous, **perīculósus, -a, -um** (17)
dark, it gets, **advesperáscit, advesperáscere** (17)
daughter, **fília, -ae,** f. (11)
day, **díēs, diéī,** m. (5, 13)
day, it is, **lúcet, lūcére** (6)
dead, **mórtuus, -a, -um** (16)
dearest, **cāríssimus, -a, -um** (16)
defend, to, **dēféndō, dēféndere** (I)
delay, to, **céssō, cessáre** (14)
depart, to, **discédō, discédere** (9)
din, **frágor, fragóris,** m. (4)

direction, **pars, pártis**, gen. pl., **pártium**, f. (13)

distance, in the, **prócul**, adv. (15)

distant, to be, **ábsum, abésse** (11)

distinguished, **praeclárus, -a, -um** (13)

ditch, **fóssa, -ae**, f. (12)

do, to, **ágō, ágere** (8, 14), **fáciō, fácere** (1)

do?, What does..., **Quid fácit...?** (1)

do nothing, to, **céssō, cessáre** (14)

dog, **cánis, cánis**, m./f. (12)

doing?, What is..., **Quid fácit...?** (1)

Don't...! **Nṓlī!/Nōlíte!** + infinitive (9)

door, **iánua, -ae**, f. (9)

doorkeeper, **iánitor, iānitóris**, m. (9)

down from, **dē**, prep. + abl. (16)

drag, to, **tráhō, tráhere** (6, 12)

drag out, to, **éxtrahō, extráhere** (14)

drive, to, **ágō, ágere, ágere** (8, 14), **íncitō, incitáre** (10)

drive off/back, to, **repéllō, repéllere** (5)

driver, **raedárius, -ī**, m. (10)

dust, **púlvis, púlveris**, m. (15)

dwell, to, **hábitō, habitáre** (1)

E

each, **ómnis, -is, -e** (6)

eight, **óctō** (15)

eleventh, **ūndécimus, -a, -um** (17)

embrace, **compléxus, -ūs**, m. (9)

embrace, in an, **compléxū** (9)

emperor, **prínceps, príncipis**, m. (7)

energetic, **strénuus, -a, -um** (2)

enter, to, **íntrō, intráre** (8)

escape, to, **effúgiō, effúgere** (11)

even, **étiam**, adv. (1, 6, 13)

every, **ómnis, -is, -e** (6, 18)

everyone, **ómnēs** (6)

everything, **ómnia** (6)

everything that, **ómnia quae** (6)

exclaim, to, **exclámō, exclāmáre** (10)

F

fall, to, **cádō, cádere** (3)

fall down, to, **cóncidō, concídere** (14)

famous, **praeclárus, -a, -um** (13)

far (off), **prócul**, adv. (15)

farm manager, **vílicus, -ī**, m. (11)

fast, very, **celérrimē**, adv. (14)

father, **páter, pátris**, m. (6, 11)

fault, **cúlpa, -ae**, f. (14)

fear, to, **tímeō, timḗre** (5)

field, **áger, ágrī**, m. (2)

fiercely, **feróciter**, adv. (13)

fifty, **quīnquāgíntā** (15)

find, to, **invéniō, inveníre** (12)

fishpond, **piscína, -ae**, f. (3)

five, **quínque** (15)

food, **cíbus, -ī**, m. (6)

foot, **pēs, pédis**, m. (13)

footprint, **vēstígium, -ī**, n. (12, 15)

for, **nam**, conj. (8)

forehead, **frōns, fróntis**, f. (12)

forest, **sílva, -ae**, f. (5)

former, the, **ílle, ílla, íllud** (11, 15, 16)

four, **quáttuor** (15)

friend, **amíca, -ae**, f. (2), **amícus, -ī**, m. (3), **hóspes, hóspitis**, m./f. (16)

frighten, to, **térreō, terrḗre** (4)

frightened, **pertérritus, -a, -um** (5)

from, **ā** or **ab**, prep. + abl. (13), **ē** or **ex**, prep. + abl. (2, 5, 9)

From where...? **Únde...?** adv. (12)

full, **plḗnus, -a, -um** (11)

G

garden, **hórtus, -ī**, m. (3)

gate, **pórta, -ae**, f. (11)

gently, **plácidē**, adv. (14)

get up, to, **súrgō, súrgere** (6)

gets dark, it, **advesperáscit, advesperáscere** (17)

girl, **puélla, -ae**, f. (1)

glad, **laétus, -a, -um** (1)

glad, to be, **gaúdeō, gaudḗre** (14)

go, to, **éō, íre** (7, 17)

Go away! **Ábī!/Abíte!** (3)

go away, to, **ábeō, abíre** (3, 9) **discḗdō, discḗdere** (9)

go back, to, **rédeō, redíre** (7)

go down, to, **dēscéndō, dēscéndere** (4)

go into, to, **íntrō, intráre** (8)

go out, to, **éxeō, exíre** (5)

go past, to, **praetéreō, praeteríre** (15)
good, **bónus, -a, -um** (12)
Goodbye! **Válē!/Valéte!** (9)
grab hold of, to, **arrípiō, arrípere** (5, 9)
great, **mágnus, -a, -um** (4)
Greek, **Graécus, -a, -um** (17)
Greeks, the, **Graécī, -órum**, m. pl. (I)
greet, to, **salútō, salūtáre** (7)
Greetings! **Sálvē!/Salvéte!** (7)
groan, to, **gémō, gémere** (3)
guard, to, **custódiō, custōdíre** (17)
guest, **hóspes, hóspitis**, m./f. (16)

H

habit (of), to be in the, **sóleō, solére** + infin. (10)
half-asleep, **sēmisómnus, -a, -um** (9)
hand over, to, **trádō, trádere** (7)
happens, (it), **áccidit, accídere** (14)
happy, **laétus, -a, -um** (1)
hard, **strénuē**, adv. (6, 13)
have, to, **hábeō, habére** (10)
he, **ílle** (11, 15, 16), **is** (2, 7)
head for, to, **pétō, pétere** (5)
hear, to, **aúdiō, audíre** (4)
Hello! **Sálvē!/Salvéte!** (7)
help, **auxílium, -ī**, n. (5,15)
Help! **Fer/Férte auxílium!** (5)
help, to, **ádiuvō, adiuváre** (6)
her, **éam** (9, 16), **éius** (2)
her (own), **súus, -a, -um** (9)
here, **hīc**, adv. (9, 13)
herself, **ípsa** (6, 10)
hide, to, **célō, cēláre** (11)
him, **éum** (5)
himself, **ípse** (6, 10), **sē** (11)
hinder, to, **impédiō, impedíre** (11)
his (own), **súus, -a, -um** (9)
hit, to, **fériō, feríre** (16)
hold, to, **hábeō, habére** (10), **téneō, tenére** (9)
horse, **équus, -ī**, m. (10)
host, **hóspes, hóspitis**, m./f. (16)
hour, **hóra, -ae**, f. (9)
house, country, **vílla, -ae**, f. (1)
How...! **Quam...!** adv. (13)
How...? **Quam...?** adv., **Quō īnstrūméntō...?**
    Quómodo...? adv. (12)

How many...? **Quot...?** (15)
however, **támen**, adv. (6, 13)
hundred, five, **quīngéntī, -ae, -a** (15)
hundred, one, **céntum** (15)
Hurray! **Eúgepae!** (7)
hurry, to, **festínō, festīnáre** (9)
husband, **vir, vírī**, m. (3, 11)

I

I, **égo** (5)
idle, to be, **céssō, cessáre** (14)
if, **sī**, conj. (5)
ignorant, to be, **nésciō, nescíre** (9)
immediately, **státim**, adv. (5, 13)
in, **in**, prep. + abl. (1, 9)
in a loud voice, **mágnā vóce** (4)
in front of, **ápud**, prep. + acc. (16)
in this way, **íta**, adv. (3, 13)
in three days, **tríbus diébus** (12, 13)
in vain, **frústrā**, adv. (14)
In what manner/way...? **Quómodo...?**
    adv. (12)
Indeed! **Íta vérō!** adv. (3, 13)
inn, **caupóna, -ae**, f. (17)
innkeeper, **caúpō, caupónis**, m. (17)
instrument...? With what,
    Quō īnstrūméntō...? (12)
intend, to, **in ánimō habére** (16)
interrupt, to, **interpéllō, interpelláre** (8)
into, **in**, prep. + acc. (3, 9)
is, (he/she/it), **est** (1)
is able, (he/she/it), **pótest** (5)
Italy, **Itália, -ae**, f. (1)
its, **éius** (2)

J

joke, **iócus, -ī**, m. (16)
journey, **íter, itíneris**, n. (10, 13, 15)

K

keep quiet, to, **quiéscō, quiéscere** (13)
know, not to, **nésciō, nescíre** (9)
know, to, **scíō, scíre** (16)

L

lady of the house, **dómina, -ae,** f. (17)
large, **mágnus, -a, -um** (4)
laugh, **rísus** (13)
laugh, with a loud, **mágnō rísū** (13)
laugh (at), to, **rídeō, rīdére** (3)
lazy, **ignávus, -a, -um** (5)
lead, to, **dúcō, dúcere** (7)
leave behind, to, **relínquō, relínquere** (16)
letter, **epístula, -ae,** f. (7)
letter (of the alphabet), **líttera, -ae,** f. (12)
light, it is, **lúcet, lūcére** (6)
light two-wheeled carriage, **císium, -ī,** n. (14, 15)
like, to, **ámō, amáre** (4)
listen to, to, **aúdiō, audíre** (4)
live, to, **hábitō, habitáre** (1)
load, **ónus, óneris,** n. (15)
long, **lóngus, -a, -um** (15)
long time, for a, **díū,** adv. (15)
look after, to, **cúrō, cūráre** (6)
Look (at...)! **Écce!** (1)
look at, to, **spéctō, spectáre** (7)
look for, to, **pétō, pétere** (5)
look out for, to, **exspéctō, exspectáre** (15)
loud laugh, with a, **mágnō rísū** (13)
loud voice, with a, **mágnā vóce** (4)
love, to, **ámō, amáre** (4)

M

make, to, **fáciō, fácere** (1)
man, **vir, vírī,** m. (3, 11)
man, old, **sénex, sénis,** m. (I)
manager, farm, **vílicus, -ī,** m. (11)
manner...?, In what, **Quómodo...?** adv. (12)
many, **múltī, -ae, -a** (3)
master, **dóminus, -ī,** m. (11)
me, **mē** (4)
me, to/for, **míhi** (8)
me, with, **mécum** (9)
means...?, By what, **Quō īnstrūméntō...?** (12)
meanwhile, **intéreā,** adv. (10, 13)
messenger, **núntius, -ī,** m. (7)
mind, **ánimus, -ī,** m. (16)
mine, **méus, -a, -um** (7)
miserable, **míser, mísera, míserum** (9)

mistaken, to be, **érrō, erráre** (5)
mistress, **dómina, -ae,** f. (17)
moment, at that, **tum,** adv. (4, 13)
moment, at that very, **éō ípsō témpore** (10)
moreover, **praetéreā,** adv. (15)
mother, **máter, mátris,** f. (6, 11)
motionless, **immóbilis, -is, -e** (12)
move, to, **móveō, movére** (14)
moved, **commótus, -a, -um** (14)
murmur, **múrmur, múrmuris,** n. (15)
mutter, to, **mússō, mussáre** (11)
my, **méus, -a, -um** (7)

N

name, **nómen, nóminis,** n. (1, 15)
name, by, **nómine** (1)
Naples, **Neápolis, Neápolis,** f. (15)
narrator, **nārrátor, nārrātóris,** m. (8)
near, **ad,** prep. + acc. (15), **própe,** prep. + acc. (5, 9)
necessary, **necésse,** adv. or indeclinable adj. (6)
neighboring, **vīcínus, -a, -um** (1)
neither...nor, **néque...néque,** conj. (5)
nevertheless, **támen,** adv. (6, 13)
new, **nóvus, -a, -um** (16)
next, **deínde,** adv. (8, 13)
night, **nox, nóctis,** gen. pl., **nóctium,** f. (11)
night, at, **nócte** (12)
night, that, **íllā nócte** (11)
nine, **nóvem** (15)
ninth, **nónus, -a, -um** (16)
no, **núllus, -a, -um** (9)
No! **Mínimē!** adv. (3, 13)
no longer, **nōn iam,** adv. (2, 13)
no one, **némō, néminis,** m./f. (9)
noise, **frágor, frāgóris,** m. (4)
not, **nōn,** adv. (2, 13)
not any, **núllus, -a, -um** (9)
Not at all! **Mínimē!** adv. (3, 13)
not to wish/want, **nólō, nólle** (5, 17)
not yet, **nóndum,** adv. (6, 13)
nothing, **níhil** (4)
nothing, to do, **céssō, cessáre** (14)
now, **iam,** adv. (1, 8, 13), **nunc,** adv. (6, 13)
number, **númerus, -ī,** m. (11)

O

often, **saépe**, adv. (2, 13)
Oh dear me! **Ō mē míseram!** (9)
Oh no! **Éheu!** interj. (7)
old man, **sénex, sénis**, m. (I)
olive grove, **olīvétum, -ī**, n. (14, 15)
on, **in**, prep. + abl. (1, 9)
on a journey, **in itínere** (10)
one, **únus, -a, -um** (15)
one…another, **álius…álius** (10)
one (of two), **álter, áltera, álterum** (1)
one…the other, the, **álter…álter** (16)
oneself, **sē** (11)
only, **tántum**, adv. (15)
open, to, **apériō, aperíre** (16)
open space, **área, -ae**, f. (11)
order, to, **iúbeō, iubére** (10)
other, **álius, ália, áliud** (10), **álter, áltera, álterum** (1)
other (of two), the, **álter, áltera, álterum** (1)
our, **nóster, nóstra, nóstrum** (14)
out of, **ē** or **ex**, prep. + abl. (2, 5, 9)
outer garment, woman's, **stóla, -ae**, f. (10)
overseer, **vílicus, -ī**, m. (11)
owner, **dóminus, -ī**, m. (11)
ox, **bōs, bóvis**, m./f. (15)

P

palla, **pálla, -ae**, f. (10)
parent, **párēns, paréntis**, m./f. (11)
part, **pars, pártis**, gen. pl., **pártium**, f. (13)
peacefully, **plácidē**, adv. (14)
peasant, **rústicus, -ī**, m. (13)
people, **hóminēs, hóminum**, m. pl. (15)
perhaps, **fortásse**, adv. (15)
pest, **moléstus, -ī**, m. (3)
picture, **pictúra, -ae**, f. (1)
place, to, **pónō, pónere** (10)
play, to, **lúdō, lúdere** (16)
play ball, to, **pílā lúdere** (16)
Pompeii, **Pompéiī, Pompeiórum**, m. pl.
Poor me! **Ō mē míseram!** (9)
prank, **iócus, -ī**, m. (16)
prank, as a, **per iócum** (16)
prepare, to, **párō, paráre** (5)

prepared, **parátus, -a, -um** (10)
presently, **mox**, adv. (6, 13)
prevent, to, **impédiō, impedíre** (11)
promise, to, **prōmíttō, prōmíttere** (9)
pull, to, **tráhō, tráhere** (6, 12)
purple-bordered toga, **tóga praetéxta, tógae praetéxtae**, f. (10)
put, to, **pónō, pónere** (10)
put on, to, **índuō, indúere** (8)

Q

quickly, **celériter**, adv. (8, 13)
quickly, most/very, **celérrimē**, adv. (14)
quiet!, Be, **Tácē!/Tacéte** (9)
quiet, to be, **táceō, tacére** (9)
quiet, to keep, **quiéscō, quiéscere** (13)

R

rage, in a, **írā commótus** (14)
rash, **temerárius, -a, -um** (5)
reach, to, **advéniō, adveníre** (5)
read, to, **légō, légere** (1)
ready, **parátus, -a, -um** (10)
ready, to get, **párō, paráre** (5)
recall, to, **révocō, revocáre** (7)
receive, to, **excípiō, excípere** (5, 16)
reckless, **temerárius, -a, -um** (5)
region, **pars, pártis**, gen. pl., **pártium**, f. (13)
rejoice, to, **gaúdeō, gaudére** (14)
remain, to, **máneō, manére** (9)
repeatedly, **idéntidem**, adv. (13)
reply, to, **respóndeō, respondére** (5)
rest, to, **quiéscō, quiéscere** (13)
return, to, **rédeō, redíre** (7)
rise, to, **súrgō, súrgere** (6)
road, **vía, -ae**, f. (10)
rod, **vírga, -ae**, f. (13)
Roman, **Rōmánus, -a, -um** (1)
Romans, the, **Rōmánī, -órum**, m. pl. (III)
Rome, **Róma, -ae**, f. (7)
Rome, to, **Rómam** (7)
room, **cubículum, -ī**, n. (8, 15)
rouse, to, **éxcitō, excitáre** (8)
rumble, **múmur, múrmuris**, n. (15)

run, to, **cúrrō, cúrrere** (2)
run away, to, **effúgiō, effúgere** (11)

S

safe, **sálvus, -a, -um** (5)
safe and sound, **incólumis, -is, -e** (14)
said, (he/she), **ínquit** (7)
same, the, **ídem, éadem, ídem** (3)
same time, at the, **símul,** adv. (9, 13)
says, (he/she), **ínquit** (7)
scent of, to catch the, **olfáciō, olfácere** (12)
scold, to, **reprehéndō, reprehéndere** (6)
second, **álter, áltera, álterum** (1), **secúndus, -a, -um** (9)
second time, a, **íterum,** adv. (8, 13)
see, to, **vídeō, vidére** (4)
seek, to, **pétō, pétere** (5)
seize, to, **arrípiō, arrípere** (5)
-self, -selves, **ípse, ípsa, ípsum** (6, 10), **sē** (11)
senator, **senátor, senātóris,** m. (7)
send, to, **míttō, míttere** (9)
seven, **séptem** (15)
seventh, **séptimus, -a, -um** (13)
shaky, **īnfírmus, -a, -um** (4)
she, **ílla** (11, 15, 16)
she-wolf, **lúpa, -ae,** f. (II)
short, **brévis, -is, -e** (2)
short time, in a, **brévī témpore** (2, 12)
shout, to, **clámō, clāmáre** (3)
shout out, to, **exclámō, exclāmáre** (10)
shout(ing), **clámor, clāmóris,** m. (5)
silence, **siléntium, -ī,** n. (15)
silently, **tácitē,** adv. (9, 13)
sister, **sóror, soróris,** f. (11)
sit, to, **sédeō, sedére** (1)
six, **sex** (15)
skill, **ars, ártis,** gen. pl., **ártium,** f. (14)
sky, **caélum, -ī,** n. (17)
slave, **sérvus, -ī,** m. (3)
slave-woman, **ancílla, -ae,** f. (6)
sleep, to, **dórmiō, dormíre** (4)
slow, **tárdus, -a, -um** (15)
slowly, **léntē,** adv. (2, 13)
smell, to, **olfáciō, olfácere** (12)
smile, **rísus, -ūs,** m. (13)
smile, to, **rídeō, rīdére** (3)

snatch, to, **arrípiō, arrípere** (5)
sniff, to, **olfáciō, olfácere** (12)
so, **íta,** adv. (3, 13)
some...others, **áliī...áliī** (9)
son, **fílius, -ī,** m. (11)
soon, **brévī témpore** (2, 12), **mox,** adv. (6, 13)
space, open, **área, -ae,** f. (11)
spend the night, to, **pernóctō, pernoctáre** (17)
spin wool, to, **lánam tráhere** (6)
spur on, to, **íncitō, incitáre** (10)
staff, **báculum, -ī,** n. (10, 15)
stand, to, **stō, stáre** (10)
statue, **státua, -ae,** f. (3)
stay, to, **máneō, manére** (9)
stealthily, **fúrtim,** adv. (4, 13)
stick, **báculum, -ī,** n. (10, 15), **vírga, -ae,** f. (13)
stick, to, **haéreō, haerére** (14)
still, **adhúc,** adv. (5, 13)
stola, **stóla, -ae,** f. (10)
stream, **rívus, -ī,** m. (5)
street, **vía, -ae,** f. (10)
strenuously, **strénuē,** adv. (6, 13)
strike, to, **fériō, feríre** (16)
stupid, **fátuus, -a, -um** (13)
suddenly, **súbitō,** adv. (3, 13)
summer, **aéstās, aestátis,** f. (1)
summer, in the, **aestáte** (1)
switch, **vírga, -ae,** f. (13)

T

take, to, **dúcō, dúcere** (7)
take care of, to, **cúrō, cūráre** (6)
take out, to, **éxtrahō, extráhere** (14)
teach, to, **dóceō, docére** (6)
ten, **décem** (15)
terrified, **pertérritus, -a, -um** (5)
terrify, to, **térreō, terrére** (4)
that, **ílle, ílla, íllud** (11, 15, 16), **quī, quae, quod** (1, 3, 14)
that night, **íllā nócte** (11)
them, **éōs** (5)
then, **deínde,** adv. (8, 13), **tum,** adv. (4, 13)
there, **íbi,** adv. (5, 13)
therefore, **ígitur,** conj. (4), **ítaque,** adv. (16)
thousand, one, **mílle** (15)
three, **trēs, trēs, tría** (13, 15)

threshing floor, **área, -ae,** f. (11)
through, **per,** prep. + acc. (6, 9)
throw, to, **iáciō, iácere** (10)
thus, **íta,** adv. (3, 13)
time, **témpus, témporis,** n. (2, 8, 12, 15)
time, in a short, **brévī témpore** (2, 12)
tired, **dēféssus, -a, -um** (2)
to(ward), **ad,** prep. + acc. (2, 9)
to Rome, **Rómam** (7)
today, **hódiē,** adv. (2, 13)
toga, **tóga, -ae,** f. (8)
toga with purple border, **tóga praetéxta, tógae praetéxtae,** f. (10)
together, **símul,** adv. (9, 13)
tomorrow, **crās,** adv. (10, 13)
too, **praetéreā,** adv. (15)
to(ward), **ad,** prep. + acc. (2, 9)
trace, **vēstígium, -ī,** n. (12, 15)
track, **vēstígium, -ī,** n. (12, 15)
travel, to, **íter fácere** (13)
tree, **árbor, árboris,** f. (1)
Trojan, **Troiánus, -a, -um** (I)
Trojans, the, **Troiánī, -órum,** m. pl. (I)
troublesome, **moléstus, -a, -um** (4)
Troy, **Tróia, -ae,** f. (I)
trunk, **císta, -ae,** f. (10)
try, to, **témptō, temptáre** (9)
tunic, **túnica, -ae,** f. (8)
turn, to, **vértō, vértere** (16)
turn aside, to, **dēvértō, dēvértere** (14)
two, **dúo, dúae, dúo** (15)

U

under, **sub,** prep. + abl. (1, 9)
unhappy, **míser, mísera, míserum** (9)
unhurt, **incólumis, -is, -e** (14)
unwilling, to be, **nólō, nólle** (5, 17)
urge on, to, **íncitō, incitáre** (10)
us, **nōs** (8)
us, for, **nóbīs** (9)
us, with, **nōbíscum** (16)

V

vehicle, **vehículum, -ī,** n. (13, 15)
vineyard, **vínea, -ae,** f. (12)

voice, **vōx, vócis,** f. (4)
voice, in a loud, **mágnā vóce** (4)

W

wagon, **plaústrum, -ī,** n. (15)
wait (for), to, **máneō, manére** (9)
wait for, to, **exspéctō, exspectáre** (15), **máneō, manére** (9)
wake (someone) up, to, **éxcitō, excitáre** (8)
walk, to, **ámbulō, ambuláre** (2)
wander, to, **érrō, erráre** (5)
want, to, **vólo, vélle** (5, 17)
want, (you), **vīs** (16)
wants, (he/she), **vult** (5, 17)
warm, **cálidus, -a, -um** (5)
was, (he/she/it), **érat** (13)
watch, to, **obsérvō, observáre** (6), **spéctō, spectáre** (7)
Watch out (for)! **Cávē!/Cavéte!** (4, 13)
watch out (for), to, **cáveō, cavére** (4, 13)
water, **áqua, -ae,** f. (6)
way, in this, **íta,** adv. (3, 13)
way...?, In what, **Quómodo...?** adv. (12)
we, **nōs** (8)
weak, **īnfírmus, -a, -um** (4)
wear, to, **gérō, gérere** (10)
weep, to, **lácrimō, lacrimáre** (9)
weeping, **lácrimāns** (9)
welcome, to, **excípiō, excípere** (5, 16), **salútō, salūtáre** (7)
well, **béne,** adv. (2)
What...? **Quid...?** (1, 4)
What does...do? **Quid fácit...?** (1)
What sort of...? **Quális...? Quális...? Quále...?** (4)
wheel, **róta, -ae,** f. (15)
when, **úbi,** conj. (5)
When...? **Quándō...?** adv. (12)
where, **úbi,** conj. (1)
Where...? **Úbi...?** adv. (10, 12)
where...?, From, **Únde...?** adv. (12)
Where...to? **Quō...?** adv. (4)
which, **quī, quae, quod** (1, 3, 14)
while, **dum,** conj. (1)
whip, to, **vérberō, verberáre** (11)
who, **quī, quae** (1, 3, 14)

Who...? (sing.) **Quis...?** (1), (pl.)
  Quī...? (6)
whole, the, **ómnis, -is, -e** (6)
Whom...? **Quem...?** (5), **Quōs...?**
  (7) **Quās...?**
whom...?, With, (sing.) **Quócum...?** (12), (pl.)
  Quibúscum (12)
Why...? **Cūr...?** adv. (1)
wicked, **sceléstus, -a, -um** (10)
wife, **úxor, uxóris,** f. (11)
willing, (he/she) is, **vult** (5, 17)
willing, to be, **vólō, vélle** (5, 17)
wish, not to, **nólō, nólle** (5, 17)
wish, to, **vólō, vélle** (5, 17)
wishes, (he/she), **vult** (5, 17)
with, **ápud,** prep. + acc. (16), **cum,** prep. +
  abl. (12)
with a loud laugh, **mágnō rísū** (13)

With whom...? (sing.) **Quócum...?** (12), (pl.)
  Quibúscum...? (12)
wolf, **lúpus, -ī,** m. (5)
woman, **fémina, -ae,** f. (3)
woods, **sílva, -ae,** f. (5)
wool, **lána, -ae,** f. (6)
wool, to spin, **lánam tráhere** (6)
work, to, **labórō, labōráre** (3)
working, **labōrántēs** (7)
worried, **sollícitus, -a, -um** (4)
wretched, **míser, mísera, míserum** (9)
write, to, **scríbō, scríbere** (1)

Y

Yes! **Íta vérō!** adv. (3, 13)
you, (sing.) **tū** (4), **tē** (4), (pl.) **vōs** (8)
your, (sing.) **túus, -a, -um** (9)

INDEX OF GRAMMAR

INDEX OF CULTURAL INFORMATION

CREDITS

The publisher gratefully acknowledges the contributions of the agencies, institutions, and photographers listed below:

Cover
(*Left*) Faustina the Younger (139–175 A.D.)
Spouse of Emperor Marc Aurel.
© Bildarchiv Precusischer Kulturbesitz/Art
Resource. (*Right*) So-called Brutus Minor.
© Alinari/Art Resource

Frontmatter
(xiv) *The Roman Campagna*, Jean-Baptiste
Camille Corot, © National Gallery Collection; By kind permission of the Trustees of
the National Gallery, London/CORBIS.

Chapter 1
(p. 4) Mosaic, Tunis, early third century
AD. © Erich Lessing/Art Resource, NY.

(p. 5) Portrait of a young boy with curls.
First century A.D. Bildarchiv Preussischer
Kulturbesitz/Art Resource, NY.

Chapter 2
(p. 8) Fragment of a Roman relief, second
century AD. Réunion des Musées
Nationaux/Art Resource, NY.

(p. 10) *Cornelia Mother of the Gracchi*,
1795, Joseph-Benoît Suvée Réunion des
Musées Nationaux/Art Resource, NY.

(p. 11) Sculpture, Pierre-Jules Cavelier.
Scala/Art Resource, NY.

Chapter 3
(p. 14) Hortus, Villa of Julia Felix, Pompeii. Jacqueline Guillot/Akg-images.

(p. 15) Bust of a Syrian slave, bronze and
lead plastic vase, Roman, 2nd century
A.D./Louvre, Paris, France/The Bridgeman Art Library.

Chapter 4
(p. 21) Courtesy of Elizabeth Lyding Will.

Chapter 5
(p. 27) Mosaic, Rome, akg-images/Tristan
Lafranchis.

(p. 29) *Episode of the* Aeneid: *The Trojan
Horse*. © The Cleveland Museum of Art,
2004. Andrew R. and Martha Holden
Jennings Fund 1974.40.

(p. 30) *Landscape with the Arrival of Aeneas
at Pallanteum* (detail), Claude Lorrain
(Claude Gellee) (1600–82)/Anglesey Abbey
Cambridgeshire, UK/The Bridgeman Art
Library.

Chapter 6
(p. 35) Glass jug, Roman, 3rd
century/Verulamium Museum, St. Albans,
Hertfordshire, UK/The Bridgeman Art
Library.

Chapter 7
(p. 40) Roman writing materials,
Roman/Verulamium Museum, St. Albans,
Hertfordshire, UK/The Bridgeman Art
Library.

(p. 43) "Mercury." Detail from the ceiling
of Palazzo Clerici, Milan, Italy. Scala/Art
Resource, NY.

(p. 44) Villa of Poppaea Sabina at Oplontis.
Bildagentur-online.com/th-foto/Alamy.

(p. 48) Panel from Cubiculum from the
bedroom of the villa of P. Fannius at
Boscoreale, Pompeii, c.50–40 B.C. (wall
painting), Roman (1st century A.D.)/Met-
ropolitan Museum of Art, New York,
USA/The Bridgeman Art Library.

(p. 51) *Aeneas Carrying Anchises*, Carle van
Loo. Scala/Art Resource, NY.

Chapter 8
(p. 55) Relief sculpture. Ancient Art &
Architecture Collection Ltd

(p. 60) *Lictor's Bearing the Bodies of His Sons
to Brutus*, Jacques-Louis David. ©
Giraudon, Louvre, Paris, France/The
Bridgeman Art Library.

(p. 61) akg-images.

Chapter 9
(p. 66) © Mimmo Jodice/CORBIS.

(p. 68) *Left*: Renato Valterza/CuboImages
srl/Alamy. *Right*: © C.M. Dixon/Ancient
Art & Architecture Collection Ltd.

Chapter 10
(p. 75) Prison cell with Roman agricultural
slaves, engraving (1866), © Index, Index,
Barcelona, Spain/The Bridgeman Art
Library.

(p. 76) Courtesy of Elizabeth Lyding
Will.

Chapter 11
(p. 85) *Romulus and Remus*, Charles de
Lafosse. Pushkin Museum, Moscow,
Russia/The Bridgeman Art Library.

(p. 86) Courtesy of Elizabeth Lyding
Will.

Chapter 12
(p. 92) Mosaic. Lauros/Giraudon, Musée
Lapidaire, Vienne, France/The Bridgeman
Art Library.

Chapter 13
(p. 101) Via Appia Antica, Rome. ©
AEP/Alamy.

Chapter 14
(p. 110) *The Oath of the Horatii*, 1784,
Jacques-Louis David. Photo © Christie's
Images, Private Collection/The Bridgeman
Art Library.

(p. 111) *The Tragedy of Lucretia*, ca.
1500–1501, Sandro Botticelli. © Isabella
Stewart Gardner Museum, Boston, MA,
USA/The Bridgeman Art Library.

Chapter 15
(p. 117) Courtesy of Elizabeth Lyding
Will.

Chapter 16
(p. 124) Roman milestone. ©SEF/Art
Resource, NY.

Chapter 17
(p. 130) Fresco. © The Metropolitan
Museum of Art/Art Resource, NY.

(p. 135) Albano Laziale, Italy. ©Scala/Art
Resource, NY.

TIMELINE